Fig. 5-1. Diminished color fidelity due to improper color temperature.

Fig. 5-2. Picture noise.

Fig. 5-4. Picture taken with an image-orthicon/vidicon camera.

Fig. 5-5. Picture taken with Plumbicon tube color camera.

Fig. 5-6. Extreme reflections depicted as white holes in picture.

Fig. 5-8. Picture taken with single tube vidicon camera.

Fig. 5-10. Contrast range depicted in a wide shot using a zoom lens.

Fig. 5-11. Contrast range depicted in an extreme closeup using a zoom lens.

TV Lighting
Handbook

No. 793
$12.95

S

TV Lighting Handbook

Dr. James K. Carroll, Director
Instructional Media Center
Mercer County Community College
Trenton, N.J.

and

Dr. Ronald E. Sherriffs, Director
Telecommunications Area
University of Oregon
Eugene, Oregon

TAB BOOKS
Blue Ridge Summit, Pa. 17214

2680922

FIRST EDITION

FIRST PRINTING—MARCH 1977

Copyright © 1977 by TAB BOOKS

Printed in the United States
of America

Library of Congress Cataloging in Publication Data

Carroll, James K
   TV lighting handbook.

   Includes index.
   1. Television--Lighting--Handbooks, manuals, etc.
I. Sherriffs, Ronald, joint author. II. Title.
TK6643.C37   791.45'02'5   76-45072
ISBN 0-8306-7793-3

46931

To our wives, Ann-Mari Carroll and Mary Sherriffs

Acknowledgments

The authors would like to thank the following individuals who played various roles in the development of this book: Dr. Robert Burdman for his assistance in testing an earlier version of the manuscript and in taking numerous photographs used during the pilot testing stage; television engineers, Mr. Frank Murphy and Mr. James Lacock, who reviewed the technical material; Mr. Garrett Smith who assisted in the photographic processing for many of the pictures found throughout the text; and Mrs. Christine Jensen and Ms. Nancy Simonsen for typing the manuscript.

Our thanks also go to the Theatre Area of the University of Oregon's Department of Speech for the use of photographs of theatre productions, the University's Division of Broadcast Services and Televised Instruction, KEZI-TV, and TelePrompTer of Oregon which provided the studio facilities in which the demonstrations were conducted. Without the help of these individuals and organizations, this book would not have become a reality.

Dr. J. K. Carroll & Dr. R. E. Sherriffs

Contents

Introduction

The increasing dependence upon the medium of television to inform, instruct, and entertain the public has created a growing need for personnel trained in media production techniques. The mastery of these production techniques serves to clarify action, reduce distractions, and add emphasis to messages.

Appropriate illumination of the subject material is one key element in television production. It provides the base for all camera coverage and subsequent electronic manipulation of images. It also sets the mood or adds aesthetic qualities which might otherwise be lacking.

The *TV Lighting Handbook* represents a text. Its purpose is to teach the student of television production essential techniques of television lighting. It is designed to be used by high schools, community colleges, professional schools, and universities actively involved in teaching television production. It may also be used by professionals in the field of television production who wish to establish in-service training programs for new employees. Commercial and Public Broadcasting stations, closed circuit instructional television units located at colleges and universities, cable companies, and industrial concerns utilizing television for personnel training are included in this category.

This book, which combines a standard text to be read by the student, a series of black and white and color photographs for purposes of illustration, and a number of response sheets for feedback, begins with four basic chapters. The four chapters cover positioning and intensity adjustments for three-light setups with a stationary subject and camera, lighting for multiple or moving cameras, and lighting for multiple subjects.

The book then introduces five chapters dealing with specific practical applications. These chapters include: Lighting for commercial and nonbroadcast color television, lighting television graphics, special lighting effects, background lighting techniques, and lighting for remote telecasts.

Advantages of such an instructional approach are numerous: (1) The reader is allowed to work at his own pace until mastery of the unit is achieved; (2) when errors are made, the reader is allowed to retrace his steps by repeating those necessary portions of the instructional sequence which were missed on the first attempt; (3) the programs are completely self-instructional, thus allowing an instructor the opportunity to concentrate on advanced techniques; (4) each chapter contains a set of objectives which identify for the reader those standards deemed critical for success in the field of television lighting; (5) instruction may take place in relatively confined areas such as study carrels, a small portion of a television or audio-visual studio, the classroom, or a room in one's home; (6) responses made on selected worksheets located throughout the program serve as sources of information for review; (7) the programs include enough comprehensive detail to enable the reader to enter the field of television production with an adequate knowledge of television lighting; and (8) the reader is provided with immediate feedback on questions posed throughout the text.

Chapter 1
Position

Chapter Objective

> *Given a realistic lighting problem in the television studio, the reader will physically position the key, back, and fill lights to achieve correct lighting of a single stationary subject located on an imaginary clock midway between 6 and 12 o'clock, with the camera positioned at 6 o'clock. The subject should be lit in a manner that contains all of the elements in the "Checklist for Proper Positioning of the Key, Back and Fill Lights" at the end of this chapter.*

The following activity will enable you to properly position *key*, *back*, and *fill* lights in a television studio to achieve a desired lighting effect.

Figure 1-1 illustrates a model which has proper *key*, *back*, and *fill* lighting. Examine the picture carefully. After completing this activity, you'll be asked to diagram a lighting setup which demonstrates a similar lighting composition.

The various lighting grids which appear throughout this chapter, as well as blank grids printed in the back of the chapter, will be used when diagraming lighting arrangements. *Such lighting arrangements will be appropriate only when a subject and camera remain in a stationary position.*

In this chapter, we will use a clock analogy. The camera will remain at 6 o'clock, in this analogy, while the subject remains midway between 6 and 12 o'clock.

Fig. 1-1. Proper key, back, and fill lighting.

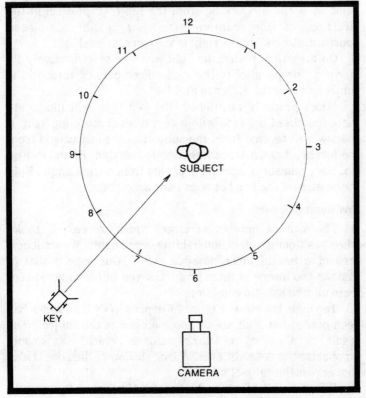

Fig. 1-2. Key light position, clock analogy.

THE KEY LIGHT

When lighting a television production it's important to position the *key* light first. The *key* is the principal source of illumination and should be placed out in front of the subject and to one side. It is used to bring out a subject's form. Refer to the light source originating from the lower left-hand side of Fig. 1-1.

Positioning

In terms of the clock analogy on a horizontal plane, the *key* would be positioned between 7 and 8 o'clock or between 4 and 5 o'clock. This position, again, is based on a camera location at the 6 o'clock position, and a subject location midway between 6 and 12 o'clock. We shall place the *key* light between 7 and 8 o'clock as shown in Fig. 1-2.

In referring to horizontal positioning, it might also be helpful to think of *key* light placement in terms of a degree point on a circle. Looking from the subject's position in the direction of the camera, the *key* would be placed approximately 45° to the right of the camera. See Fig. 1-3.

On a vertical plane, the light would be placed roughly 45° above a line parallel to the studio floor passing through the subject's eye level. Refer to Fig. 1-4.

When properly positioned, the *key* light will illuminate three-fourths of the face with a very distinct modeling light. A shadow will be cast from the subject's nose and extend from the forehead down the cheekbone to the chin. Examine Fig. 1-5. Here you see a lighting grid shot from a front angle. Note the position of the *key* between 7 and 8 o'clock.

Positioning Errors

There are a number of errors which are easy to make when positioning television lighting instruments. We shall now present a few of these possible errors. Our hope is that in making you aware of these problems, you will be able to avoid them under realistic conditions.

Too high, too close. Figure 1-6 depicts a *key* light which has been placed too high above and too close to the subject. The result is a series of dark shadows which unfavorably emphasize the deep set eyes. A long shadow of the nose is also cast across the subject's face.

Compare this picture with Fig. 1-1. If you were to duplicate this error, where would you place the *key* on a lighting grid?

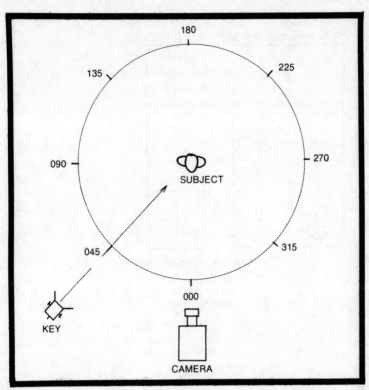

Fig. 1-3. Key light position, degree points on a circle.

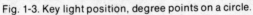

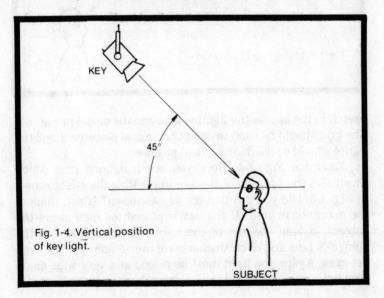

Fig. 1-4. Vertical position
of key light.

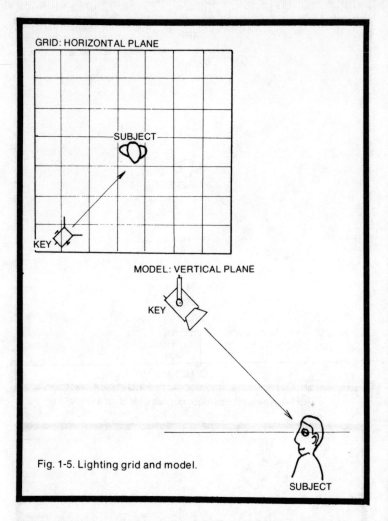

GRID: HORIZONTAL PLANE

SUBJECT

KEY

MODEL: VERTICAL PLANE

KEY

SUBJECT

Fig. 1-5. Lighting grid and model.

Sketch in the *key* on the lighting grid and the model in Fig. 1-7. The grid should be used to depict horizontal placement and the figure should be used for vertical position.

Examine Fig. 1-8. Here you see a lighting grid which illustrates the position of the *key* in creating the effect shown in Fig. 1-6. Did you position the *key* as shown? If not, think of the error illustrated. If the *key* is placed too high above the subject, a long shadow of the nose will be cast across the subject's face and dark shadows will over-emphasize the deep set eyes. Again, the light must be placed at a very wide angle above the subject's head, and close to him, in order to create

Fig. 1-6. Key placed too high and too close.

this error. The angle of the light in this position will cause shadows to extend downward. Examine both photos again.

Too low. Figure 1-9 depicts a *key* light which has been placed at an angle below eye level. The modeling effect is diminished when the *key* light is placed at this angle. The subject appears to lose form and the shadows produce a ghostly or mysterious effect. Examine the picture closely, and compare it with Fig. 1-1. Duplicate the error by placing the *key*

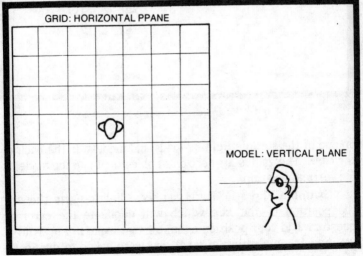

Fig. 1-7. Lighting grid and model.

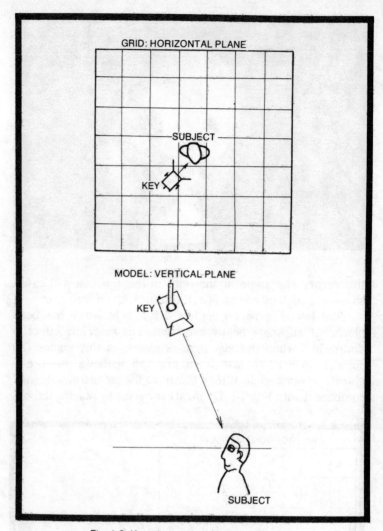

GRID: HORIZONTAL PLANE

SUBJECT

KEY

MODEL: VERTICAL PLANE

KEY

SUBJECT

Fig. 1-8. Key placed too high and too close.

on one of the sample lighting grids and models, in the back of the book. The grid is for horizontal placement and the model is for vertical position.

Examine Fig. 1-10. Here you see a lighting grid showing the position of the *key* which will duplicate the error in question. Did your positioning match that found in Fig. 1-10? If you had trouble, think of what you were asked to duplicate. You wanted to place the light low and close enough to produce

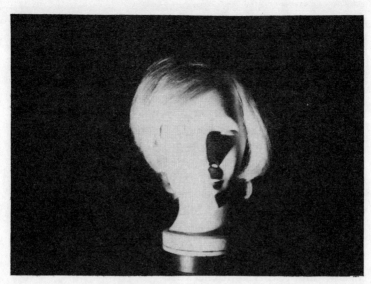

Fig. 1-9. Key placed too low.

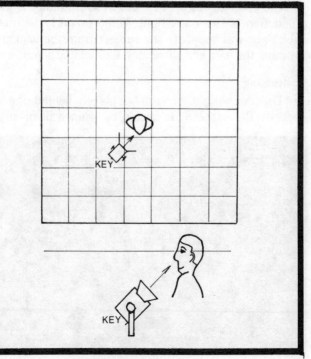

Fig. 1-10. Key placed too low.

a ghostly effect. In addition, you wanted to give the face an unfamiliar form. The critical position in this case is the angle of the *key*, which should fall below the eye level of the subject.

Review

Figure 1-11 illustrates proper placement of the *key* light. The modeling effect is evident. Examine the photo closely and then sketch in the *key* on one of the sample lighting grids and models in the end of this chapter.

Figure 1-5 depicted the correct positioning of the *key* light with its subsequent effect. If you had difficulty positioning the *key* correctly, review the earlier pages on *key* light. Before you begin, refer to the additional information list titled *Checklist for Positioning The Key Light* at the end of this chapter.

If you positioned the *key* correctly, but would like a quick review, refer to this same checklist.

THE BACK LIGHT

The second light to set when lighting a television production is the *back* light. When properly positioned, the *back* light will separate the subject from the background by rimming the hair and shoulders, thus adding depth.

Positioning

The *back* light should be placed behind the subject, opposite the camera. It should be trained primarily on the

Fig. 1-11. Key light correct.

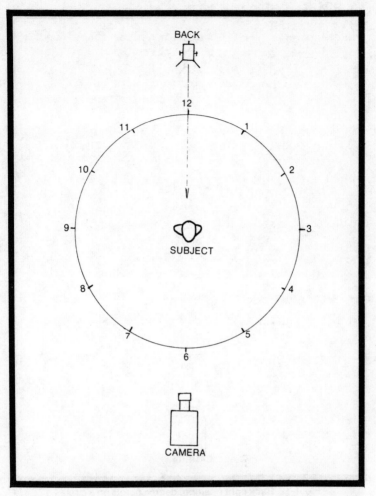

Fig. 1-12. Back light position, clock analogy.

subject's head and shoulders. Given the camera position at 6 o'clock, in our clock analogy, the *back* light would be placed at 12 o'clock. Figure 1-12 shows this arrangement.

Examine Fig. 1-13. Here you see the position of the back light in terms of degrees on a circle. The correct position in this instance is 180°. On a vertical plane, the light should be positioned at a 45° angle above a line parallel to the studio floor passing through the subject's eye level, although the small size of many television studios often dictates an angle up to 75°. See Fig. 1-14.

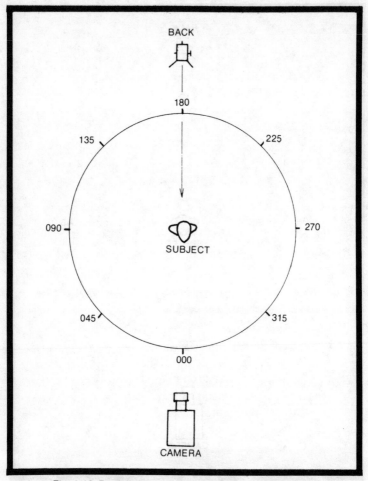

Fig. 1-13. Back light position, degree points on a circle.

Positioning Errors

When improperly positioned, the *back* light will fail to separate the subject from the background or it will cast uneven light and shadows.

Top Light. Figure 1-15 depicts a *back* light that has been placed too close to the subject. Notice that light is cast on the subject's forehead with a highlight on the tip of the subject's nose. This effect is called a *top light*. To help illustrate this effect, we have removed the *key* light.

Such a problem may be eliminated by placing the subject far out in front of the set or background. This placement allows

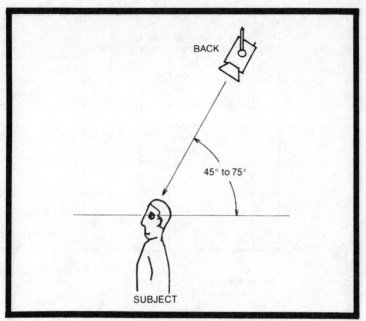

Fig. 1-14. Vertical position of back light.

the *back* light to be positioned at a proper distance behind the subject. Examine Fig. 1-15 again. Now sketch in the *back* light to duplicate the error using one of the sample lighting grids and models found at the end of this Chapter. Remember the grid represents horizontal positioning while the model represents vertical positioning.

Fig. 1-15. Back placed too close causes top light.

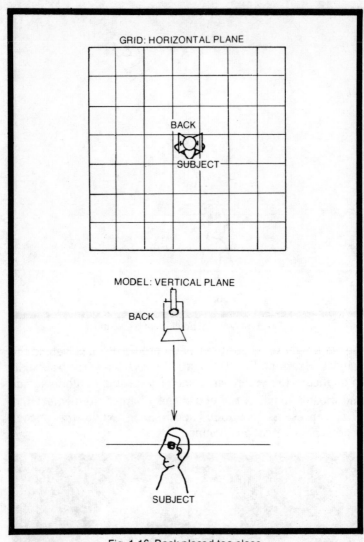

GRID: HORIZONTAL PLANE

BACK
SUBJECT

MODEL: VERTICAL PLANE

BACK

SUBJECT

Fig. 1-16. Back placed too close.

Examine Fig. 1-16. This lighting grid and model shows the position of the *back* which creates the error in question. If you were unable to duplicate the error, analyze the situation. To cause light to be cast on the subject's forehead and nose, the *back* light would have to be placed directly over and slightly out in front of the subject's head. Think about this setup.

Too far to one side. Figure 1-17 illustrates the effect the *back* light has on the subject when placed too far to one side.

Fig. 1-17. Key correct. Back too far to one side.

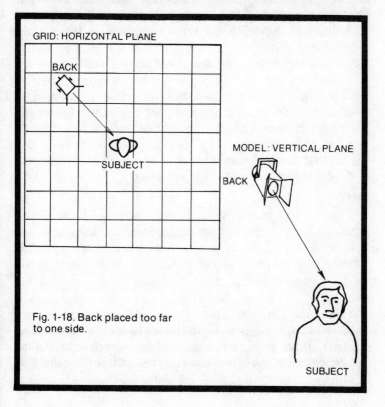

GRID: HORIZONTAL PLANE

BACK

SUBJECT

MODEL: VERTICAL PLANE

BACK

Fig. 1-18. Back placed too far
to one side.

SUBJECT

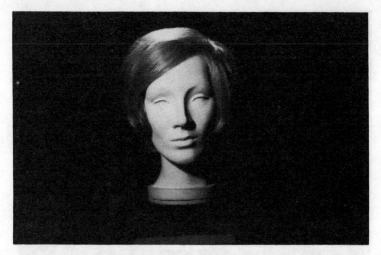

Fig. 1-19. Back positioned correctly.

One side of the subject's face is lit too brightly and the hair is lit unevenly. Compare this photograph with Fig. 1-1 which illustrates correct lighting. Again it's your turn to sketch in the *back* light to duplicate the error using one of the sample lighting grids and models in the back of the chapter. Don't forget to sketch in both horizontal and vertical positions.

Examine Fig. 1-18. Here you see a lighting grid showing the *back* light positioned to achieve the effect in question. If you had trouble, analyze the assignment. You must place the *back* light in such a position to light one side of the subject's face and in the process throw uneven lighting on the hair. This means that the *back* must be placed to one side of 12 o'clock so that light will be cast on the subject's face.

Review

Figure 1-19 shows the *back* light positioned in its proper location. We've achieved the highlighting or rimming of the hair with sufficient subject-to-background separation. Examine Fig. 1-19 closely and then sketch in the *back* light on one of the sample lighting grids and models in the back of this chapter.

Examine Fig. 1-20. This lighting grid depicts the correct position of the *back* light. If you did not locate the *back* light in the correct position, reread the section on *back* light. Before you repeat the steps listed, however, refer to the *Checklist For Positioning The Back Light* at the end of the Chapter.

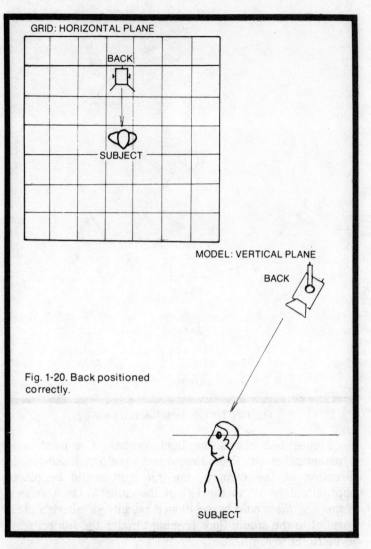

GRID: HORIZONTAL PLANE

BACK

SUBJECT

MODEL: VERTICAL PLANE

BACK

Fig. 1-20. Back positioned correctly.

SUBJECT

THE FILL LIGHT

The third and final light to position is the *fill* light. This light is a supplementary form of illumination used to *reduce* the shadow cast by the *key* light.

Positioning

Given the camera position at 6 o'clock, as depicted in Fig. 1-21, the *fill* light would be placed opposite the *key*, and in this case located between 4 and 5 o'clock.

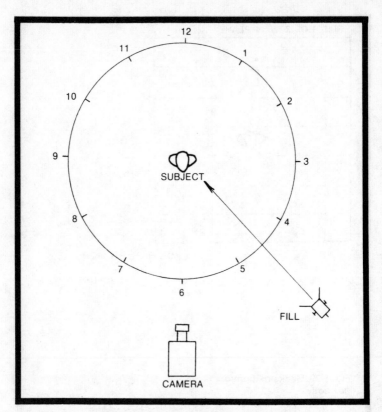

Fig. 1-21. Fill light position, clock analogy.

Figure 1-22 shows the light located at a point on a hypothetical circle. From the subject's position, looking in the direction of the camera, the *fill* light would be placed approximately 45° to the left of the camera. On a vertical plane, the *fill* should be positioned roughly 45° above a plane parallel to the studio floor passing through the subject's eye level. Refer to Fig. 1-23.

Positioning Errors

As with the *key* and *back* lights, an incorrectly positioned *fill* light can cause special problems.

Too far to one side. Examine Fig. 1-24. The picture shows the *fill* light located too far to one side. This placement casts a shadow across the front of the subject's face. Located in this position, the fill light is unable to properly perform its function of reducing or filling in the shadows cast by the *key* light.

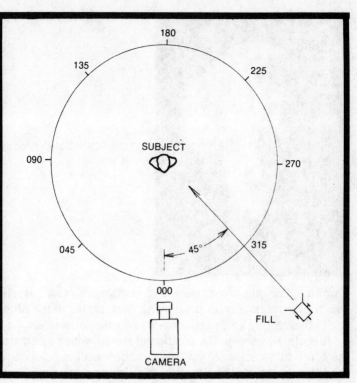

Fig. 1-22. Fill light position, degree points on a circle.

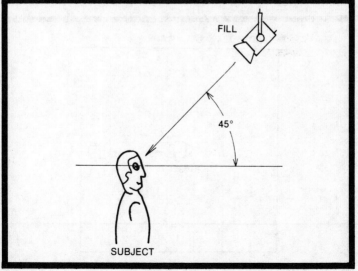

Fig. 1-23. Vertical position of fill light.

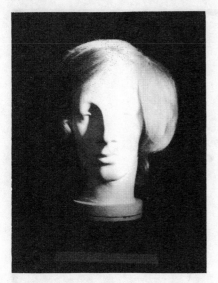

Fig. 1-24. Fill placed too far to one side.

Examine this picture closely and compare it with Fig. 1-1 which illustrates correct positioning. Now sketch in the *fill* on one of the lighting grids and models to duplicate the effect.

Figure 1-25 shows the position of the *fill* which illustrates the error in question. If you were unsuccessful in positioning the *fill*, re-examine the situation. You were asked to duplicate an error in which the shadow was cast across the front of the subject's face. To do this, the *fill* must be placed in the area of

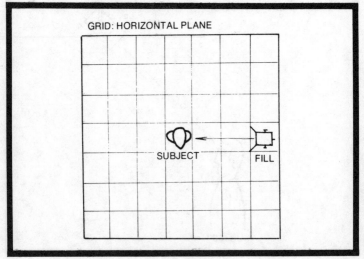

Fig. 1-25. Fill placed too far to one side.

Fig. 1-26. Key and back correct. Fill too close to 6 o'clock.

3 o'clock, which is slightly forward of its correct position between 4 and 5 o'clock. In the 3 o'clock position, a shadow will be cast across the front of the subject's face. Think about this arrangement while examining Figs. 1-25 and 1-24.

Too close to 6 o'clock. Figure 1-26 shows the results of placing the *fill* light too close to the 6 o'clock position. The end

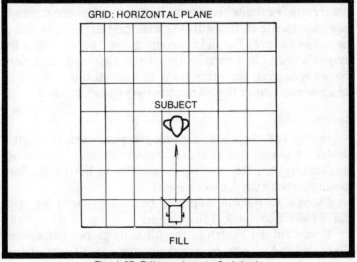

Fig. 1-27. Fill too close to 6 o'clock.

Fig. 1-28. Fill positioned correctly.

product is a very flat picture with a shadow on the far right side of the subject's face. The *fill* in this case has destroyed the modeling or three-dimensional effect achieved by the *key* light. Also note the elongated or V-shaped shadow cast by the subject's chin on her neck. Compare this picture with Fig. 1-1. Once you have compared the two, sketch in the *fill* light on one of the lighting grids and models to duplicate the error.

Figure 1-27 shows the *fill* positioned on the lighting grid to duplicate the error in question. If you charted the light incorrectly, examine the error. The picture you are trying to duplicate should be flat with a shadow cast on the right side of the subject's face. The light is coming from the left side of the subject's face. In order to throw the right side into dark shadow you must therefore keep all light off that side. To do this, you must move the *fill* close to the 6 o'clock position.

Review

In Fig. 1-28, the *fill* light is properly positioned. The light is located between the 4 and 5 o'clock position, and is approximately 45° above a plane parallel to the studio floor passing through the subject's eyes.

Place a *fill* light in its proper position on one of the grids and models in the back of this chapter.

If you did not sketch in the *fill* in its proper location, as illustrated in Fig. 1-29, review the sections on *fill* light. Before you begin, refer to the *Checklist for Positioning The Fill Light*.

Examine Fig. 1-30. Do you see any difference between this picture and Fig. 1-1? Here's a clue: The *key* is coming from the model's left-hand side. If you have learned the chapter's objective, you should be able to duplicate the effect illustrated in Fig. 1-30. Sketch in the *key*, *back*, and the *fill* lights on one of the lighting grids and models. Don't forget to note the change in positioning between the *key* and *fill*. In addition, mark in all horizontal and vertical positions.

Figure 1-31 shows the correct positioning of all three lights to achieve the effect shown in Fig. 1-30. The *key* and *fill* lights have been reversed in this instance. If you had difficulty understanding this section, review the chapter. Refer first to the three checklists for positioning the *back*, *key*, and *fill*. Once you've finished, light a subject in your television studio. Have your instructor or lighting supervisor evaluate your performance.

Checklist For Positioning The Key Light

1. The *key* is the principal source of illumination and should illuminate three-fourths of the subject's face.
2. The *key* should be placed between 4 and 5 o'clock or 7 and 8 o'clock, using a clock analogy, provided the camera remains at the 6 o'clock position. Given a point on an imaginary circle, the *key* should be placed 45° to the right of the camera, viewed from the position of the subject, facing the camera.

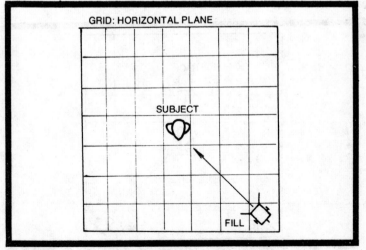

Fig. 1-29. Fill positioned correctly.

Fig. 1-30. Key and fill reversed.

3. On a vertical plane the *key* should be 45° above a line parallel to the studio floor which passes through the subject's eye level.
4. If the *key* is placed properly, a shadow should be cast from the subject's nose, and should extend from the forehead down the cheekbone to the chin.
5. Examine the eyes and cheeks of the subject. If they are in deep shadow, the *key* has probably been placed too high and too close to the subject.

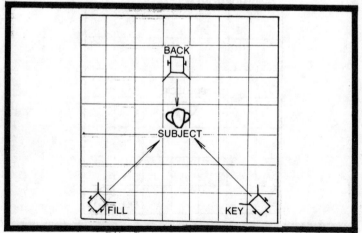

Fig. 1-31. Key and fill reversed.

6. Avoid placing the light at too low an angle. The result will be a ghostly or mysterious effect.

Checklist For Positioning The Back Light

1. The *back* light should separate the subject from the background.
2. Using a clock analogy, with the camera at 6 o'clock, the *back* should be placed at 12 o'clock and should be aimed at the subject's head and shoulders. Given a point on an imaginary circle, the *back* should be placed 180° directly behind the subject.
3. On a vertical plane, the *back* should be placed between 45° and 75° above a line parallel to the studio floor which passes through the subject's eye level. The studio size will dictate the angle used.
4. If the hair and shoulders appear to be lit unevenly and one side of the face appears too bright, the *back* may be too far to one side.
5. Do not place the *back* directly over the subject's head. When you see shadows cast on the subject's forehead, nose, and cheeks, and when dark hollows appear under the eyebrows, the light is too close. This error illustrates what is commonly referred to as a *top light*.

Checklist For Positioning The Fill Light

1. The *fill* light is a supplementary form of illumination used to reduce the shadow cast by the *key* light.
2. The *fill* should be placed opposite the *key* light either between 4 and 5 o'clock or 7 and 8 o'clock, when the camera remains at 6 o'clock. Given a point on an imaginary circle, the *fill* should be placed 45° to the left of the camera when standing in the position of the subject, facing the camera.
3. On a vertical plane, the *fill* should be placed 45° above a line parallel to the studio floor which passes through the subject's eye level.
4. If you see a shadow cast across the front of the subject's face, the *fill* may be positioned too far to one side.
5. If your picture appears too flat, and one side of the subject's face is dark, then the *fill* may be placed too close to the 6 o'clock position.

LIGHTING GRIDS AND MODELS

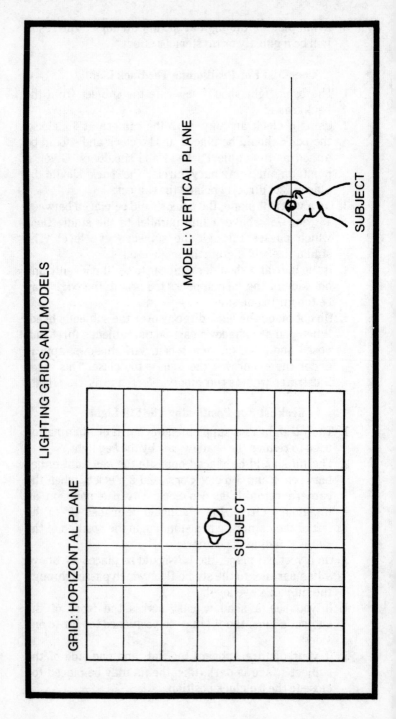

GRID: HORIZONTAL PLANE

SUBJECT

MODEL: VERTICAL PLANE

SUBJECT

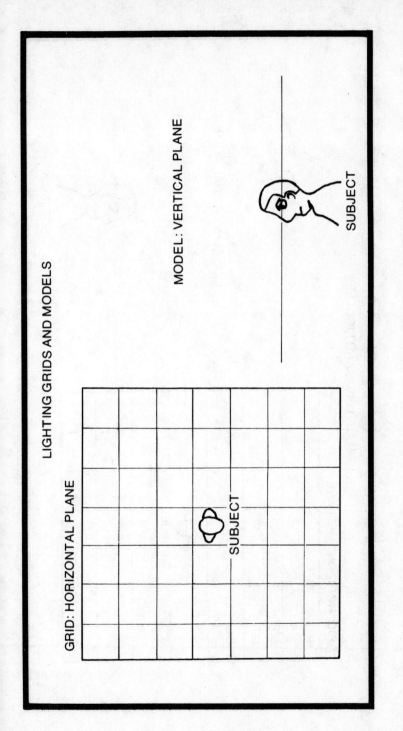

LIGHTING GRIDS AND MODELS

GRID: HORIZONTAL PLANE

SUBJECT

MODEL: VERTICAL PLANE

SUBJECT

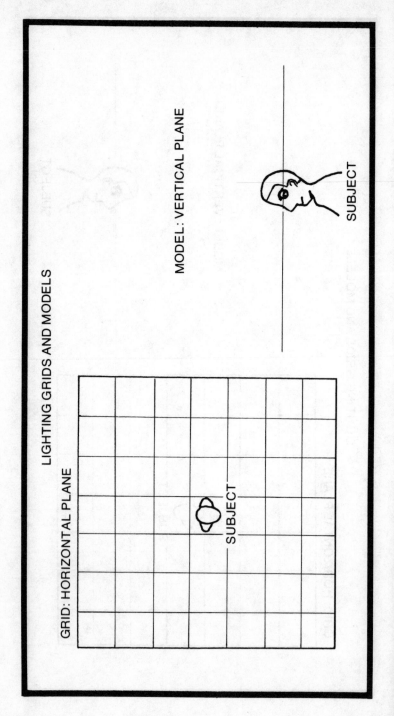

LIGHTING GRIDS AND MODELS

GRID: HORIZONTAL PLANE

SUBJECT

MODEL: VERTICAL PLANE

SUBJECT

44

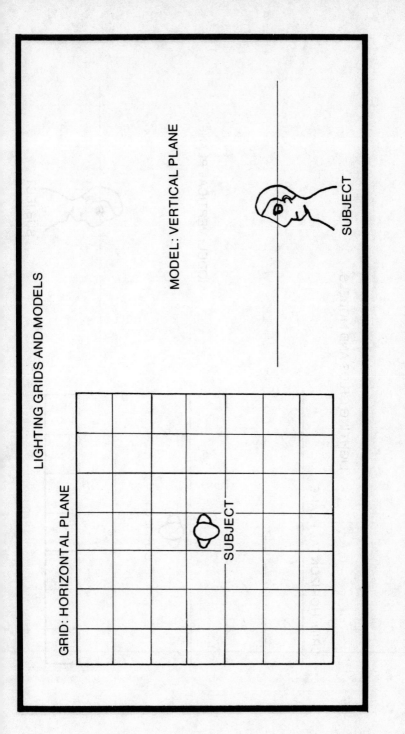

LIGHTING GRIDS AND MODELS

GRID: HORIZONTAL PLANE

SUBJECT

MODEL: VERTICAL PLANE

SUBJECT

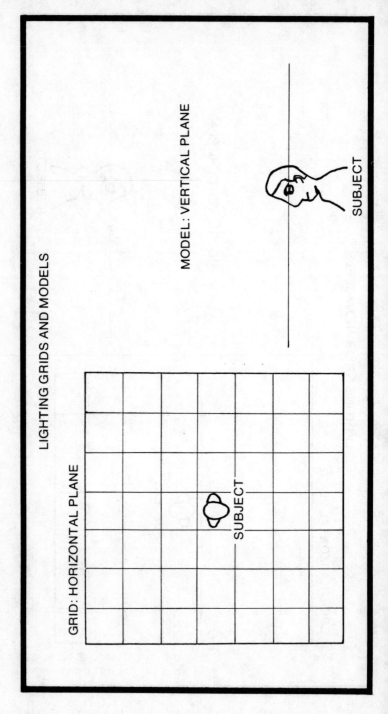

LIGHTING GRIDS AND MODELS

GRID: HORIZONTAL PLANE

SUBJECT

MODEL: VERTICAL PLANE

SUBJECT

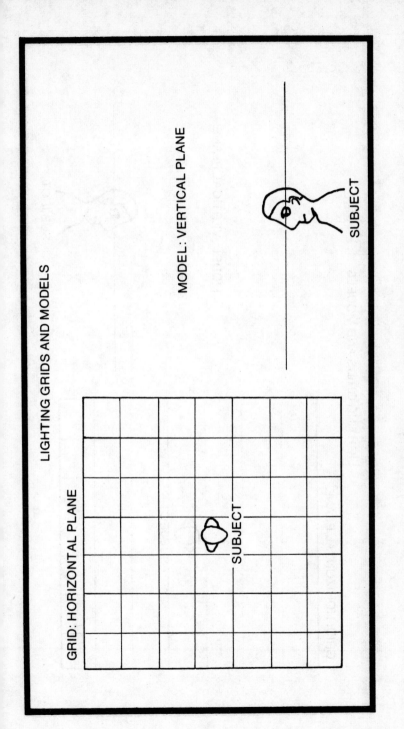

LIGHTING GRIDS AND MODELS

GRID: HORIZONTAL PLANE

SUBJECT

MODEL: VERTICAL PLANE

SUBJECT

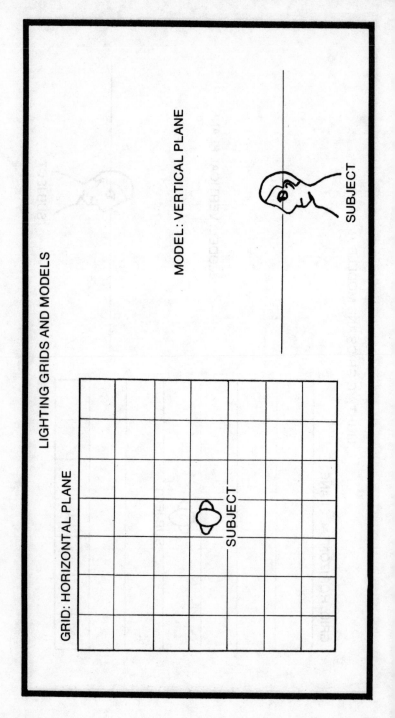

LIGHTING GRIDS AND MODELS

GRID: HORIZONTAL PLANE

SUBJECT

MODEL: VERTICAL PLANE

SUBJECT

48

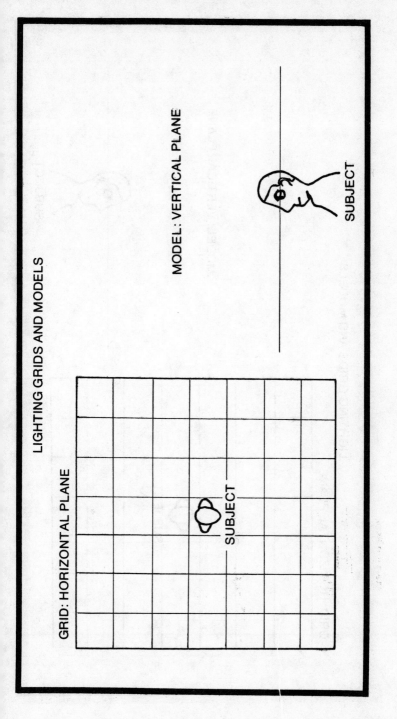

LIGHTING GRIDS AND MODELS

GRID: HORIZONTAL PLANE

SUBJECT

MODEL: VERTICAL PLANE

SUBJECT

49

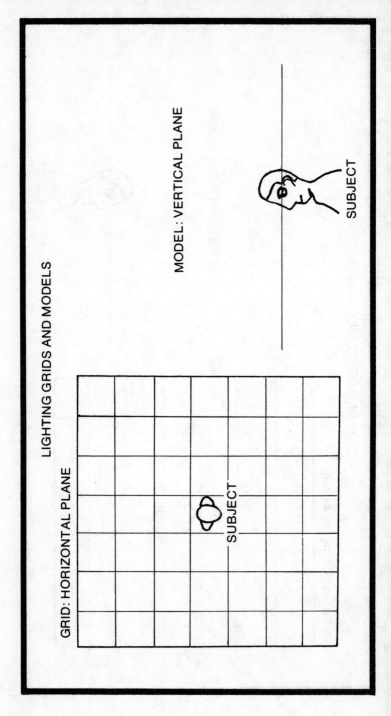

LIGHTING GRIDS AND MODELS

GRID: HORIZONTAL PLANE

SUBJECT

MODEL: VERTICAL PLANE

SUBJECT

50

Chapter 2

Intensity

Chapter Objective

Given a realistic lighting problem in the television studio, the reader will adjust the intensities of the key, back, and fill lights to achieve correct lighting of a single stationary subject located on an imaginary clock, midway between 6 and 12 o'clock with the camera positioned at 6 o'clock. The subject should be lit in a manner that contains all of the elements in the Checklist For Proper Intensity Adjustment of The Key, Back, and Fill Lights, at the end of this chapter.

The last chapter showed you how to properly position the *key*, *back*, and *fill* lights to duplicate a desired lighting effect. This chapter will enable you to recognize proper intensity adjustment of the *key*, *back*, and *fill* lights. It will also explain the reasoning behind correct intensity adjustment.

Figure 2-1 illustrates a subject with proper *key*, *back*, and *fill* lighting. The lights have been positioned correctly, and their intensities have been properly set. After completing this activity, you'll be able to select, from a series of pictures, a subject displaying equally good lighting and the ingredients which make up good lighting—correct positioning and intensity adjustment.

Fig. 2-1. Key, back, fill lights correct.

THE BACK LIGHT

When lighting a television program, light intensity becomes important. We shall begin our demonstration with the *back* light. The function of the *back* light, you will remember, is to separate the subject from the background by rimming the hair and shoulders, thus adding depth to the picture. Figure 2-2 shows the *back* light positioned behind the subject at 180° or at 12 o'clock, referring to the clock analogy.

Examine Fig. 2-1 again, but this time look at the lighting from the standpoint of intensity. All three lights are working correctly together.

At this point, let us introduce a rule of thumb for adjusting intensity: Under ideal conditions, the intensity of the *back* light should be equal to the intensity of the *key* light plus the *fill* light, and the *fill* should be two-thirds the intensity of the *key*.

This is a rule of thumb only and will vary according to studio ceiling height, distance of lighting instruments from the subject's skin and clothing, and the degree of contrast with the background. The rule does, however, give an approximation when viewing relationships among the three lights.

In more general terms, the *back* light should have the strongest intensity, the *key* light should be second, and the *fill* light third.

We shall now present a number of common errors in intensity adjustment.

Intensity Too Great

Figure 2-3 shows a situation where the *back* light is too intense. Notice that the subject seems to dominate the scene. This may represent a desired effect in a single subject set, but when multiple subjects are used, the effect is annoying and often confusing. In addition, the high contrast range between the subject and the background produces a very unnatural

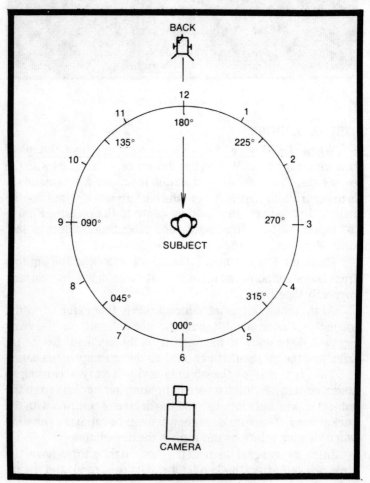

Fig. 2-2. Back light position.

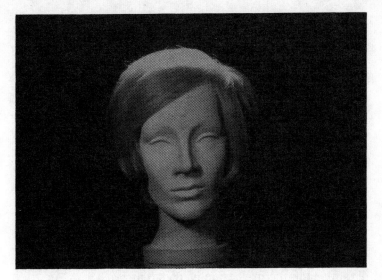

Fig. 2-3. Back too intense.

halo effect. Examine the picture carefully and compare it with Fig. 2-1.

See if you can recognize this error by examining the three pictures in Fig. 2-4. One of these photos illustrates an excess of *back* light intensity. Write down the letter of the picture you think displays the problem in question.

Photograph *c* in Fig. 2-4 illustrates the error described. If you did not choose *c*, back up and examine the three pictures

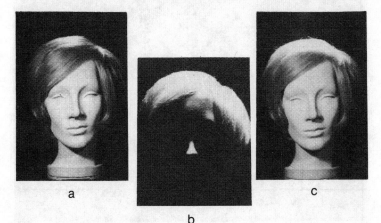

a

b

c

Fig. 2-4. Back light errors.

again. Think of the effect you're looking for. The subject should dominate the scene, and the high contrast range between the subject and the background should produce a bright halo effect.

Photographs *a* and *b* depict errors in positioning. Photograph *a* illustrates the result of placing the *back* too far to one side, while *b* illustrates a top lighting effect caused by placing the *back* light too close to the subject. Although it's true that the *back* light should be the brightest light in intensity, *c* shows a *back* light which is too intense. The halo effect is very apparent.

Intensity Too Low

Figure 2-5 illustrates the effect the *back* light has on the subject when its intensity is too low. There is a lack of adequate separation between the subject and the background. Examine this picture carefully, then compare it with Fig. 2-1.

To check your ability to recognize the error in question, examine the three photographs in Fig. 2-6. One of these photos illustrates the problem of inadequate *back* light. Write down the letter of the photo you think displays the problem.

If you chose picture *b*, you were correct. If you chose either *a* or *c*, you need some additional work. Examine each

Fig. 2-5. Back intensity too low.

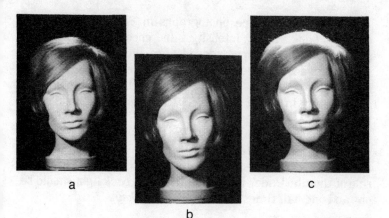

a

b

c

Fig. 2-6. Back light errors.

picture carefully. Photograph *a* illustrates correct intensity with adequate subject-to-background separation. Photograph *c* illustrates *back* light intensity which is too high. In *b*, the subject appears to blend into the background, which is the error we're looking for. Keep in mind that in correct intensity adjustment, the *back* light should equal the *key* plus *fill*.

Review

In Fig. 2-7 the *back* light is doing its job. The intensity is correct, as shown by adequate subject-to-background separation.

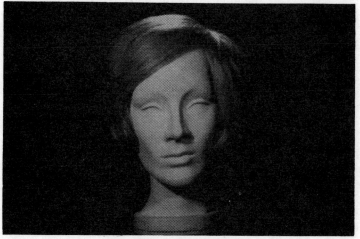

Fig. 2-7. Back intensity correct.

Examine the three photographs in Fig. 2-8. One shows correct *back* light intensity. In choosing the correct photograph remember: Under ideal conditions, the *back* light should be equal in intensity to one and one-half times the *key* light. The rule does not always work exactly, but can be used as an approximation. Now select the picture you think shows correct back light intensity in Fig. 2-8.

You should have selected *a*, the picture which shows correct *back* light intensity. If you chose a different picture, review the earlier sections of this chapter. Don't forget the rule of thumb: Under ideal conditions, the *back* light should be one and one-half times the intensity of the *key*.

THE FILL LIGHT

The next light to adjust is the *fill* light. You may recall that the *fill* light is a supplementary form of illumination used to reduce the shadow cast by the *key* light. Looking at Fig. 2-9, you can see that the *fill* light is placed between 4 and 5 o'clock or at 45° on an imaginary circle. In addition, the *fill* should be located on a vertical plane approximately 45° above a line parallel to the floor passing through the subject's eyes.

In terms of intensity, think of the following rule of thumb: Under ideal conditions, the *fill* should be two-thirds the intensity of the *key* light. Of the three lights, the *fill* provides the least intensity.

Intensity Too Great

In Fig. 2-10, the intensity of the *fill* is too great. To further illustrate the *fill's* effect on the *key*, we've added the *key* light

a

b

c

Fig. 2-8. Back light examples.

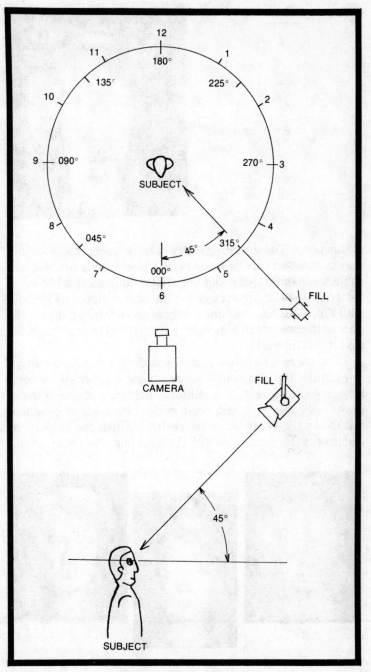

Fig. 2-9. Fill light position.

59

Fig. 2-10. Fill too intense.

at this point. The modeling effect of the *key*, especially on the cheeks, nose and above the eyes, has been eliminated, and the subject is illuminated under very flat conditions. In addition, a butterfly shadow appears under the nose. Compare Fig. 2-10 with Fig. 2-1. Then examine the three photographs in Fig. 2-11. Choose the one which illustrates a *fill* that has been adjusted at too high an intensity.

The correct selection is *a*. If you did not select correctly, re-examine the situation. Pictures *b* and *c* illustrate correct intensity adjustment. In *b*, all three lights are shown, while *c* shows only the *back* and *key* together. Photograph *a*, which illustrates the error we're interested in, finds the subject lit under very flat conditions with the modeling effect eliminated.

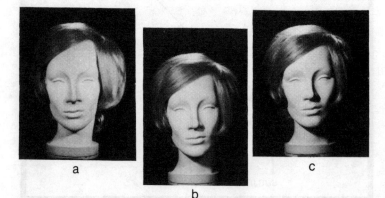

a

b

c

Fig. 2-11. Fill light examples.

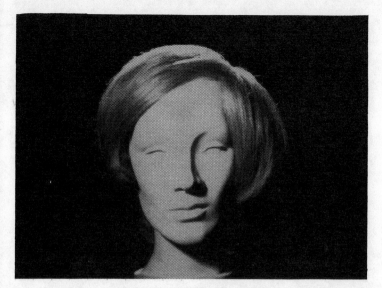

Fig. 2-12. Fill intensity too low.

Remember, the *fill* should be the least intense of the three lights. In *a*, it is the most intense.

Intensity Too Low

Figure 2-12 illustrates what happens when the intensity of the *fill* light is too low. The subject appears to be illuminated in a way that is proprotionately out of balance. There is too great a contrast between the *key* and *fill* lights, with the *key* overly dominating the arrangement. Compare Fig. 2-12 with Fig. 2-1.

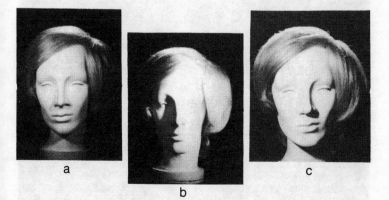

a b c

Fig. 2-13. Fill light examples.

Then examine the three pictures in Fig. 2-13. Choose the one which illustrates the *fill* light with too low an intensity.

The correct response in this instance is *c*. Those having difficulty should take additional time to compare the previous three photos. You're looking for a picture which lights the subject in a way that is proportionately out of balance. Too great a contrast exists between the *key* and *fill* lights, with the *key* dominating the arrangement. *C* is the best illustration of this error. Although the *fill* displays the least intensity, it is far less than two-thirds the intensity of the *key*. Photograph *a*, on the other hand, shows the *back* and *key* with the *key* set too low. In *b* we see an error in positioning.

Review

Figure 2-14 shows a *fill* light doing its proper job. The shadows cast by the *key* are reduced, and the modeling effect is retained. Examine the three pictures in Fig. 2-15. Only one shows the correct example of the rule: Under *ideal* conditions, the *fill* light should be equal to two-thirds the intensity of the *key* light. Again, the rule may not come out exactly as given. Select the picture which shows correct *fill* intensity relative to the *key* in Fig. 2-15.

You should have selected photograph *a*. If you chose one of the other pictures, review the section of this chapter on *fill*

Fig. 2-14. Fill intensity correct.

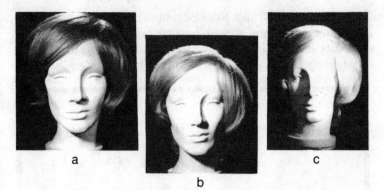

Fig. 2-15. Fill light examples.

light intensity. Photograph *b* depicts a *fill* too low in intensity, and *c* illustrates the effect of placing a *fill* at the 4 o'clock position. Keep our rule of thumb in mind.

THE KEY LIGHT

Now for the final light, the *key*. You should recall that the function of the *key* is to provide modeling light and to act as the principal source of illumination. Referring to the clock analogy in Fig. 2-16, notice that the *key* is located between the 7 and 8 o'clock positions, 45° to the right of the camera from the subject's point of reference. In addition, the key is located on a vertical plane approximately 45° above a line parallel to the studio floor passing through the subject's eyes.

From the standpoint of intensity, the *key* should be one and one-half times that of the *fill* under ideal conditions.

Intensity Too Great

Figure 2-17 shows a subject lit with too much intensity originating from the *key* light. The image is a distracting one. Contrasts on the subject's face are too great. Examine Fig. 2-17 carefully and compare it with Fig. 2-1. All three lights are being used to illustrate the effect.

Examine the three pictures in Fig. 2-18. One illustrates a *key* light with too high an intensity. Choose the correct photograph.

If you chose *b*, you're correct. If not, take a look at the three photos once again. The effect you're looking for is one in which there is too great a light-dark contrast on the subject's face. Only *b* illustrates this. Remember the rule, under ideal conditions, the *key* should be one and one-half times the intensity of the *fill*, and the *key* plus *fill* should equal the *back*. Photograph *b* shows the *key* with the greatest intensity of the

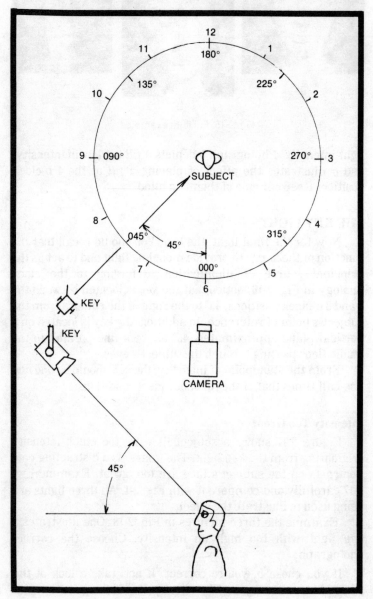

Fig. 2-16. Key light position.

Fig. 2-17. Key too intense.

three. Photograph *a* shows correct *key* intensity, while *c* illustrates a *key* placed too close to the 9 o'clock position.

Intensity Too Low

Figure 2-19 shows the subject in too little *key* light. The modeling effect is almost totally lost in this picture. Examine Fig. 2-19 carefully and compare it with Fig. 2-1. Now, choose from the three examples provided in Fig. 2-20 the one which illustrates a *key* light with too low an intensity.

Photograph *c* is the correct response. If you didn't select *c*, re-examine the three pictures. The error you're attempting to

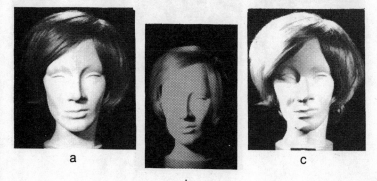

a

b

c

Fig. 2-18. Key light examples.

Fig. 2-19. Key intensity too low.

find is one in which the modeling effect is almost totally lost because of too little *key* intensity. The portion of the subject's face normally covered by the *key* should appear dimmer in this instance. Only *c* illustrates this effect. Photograph *a* depicts a *key*, alone, positioned too high, and *b* illustrates a *key*, also alone, positioned too low.

Review

In Fig. 2-21 the intensity of all three lights, *back, key,* and *fill,* are correct once again.

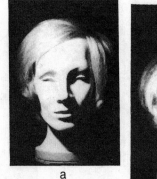

a

b

c

Fig. 2-20. Key light examples.

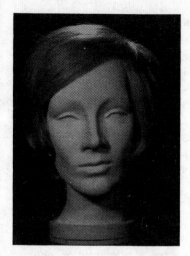

Fig. 2-21. Key, back, fill correct.

To review the rule of thumb: Under *ideal* conditions, the *key* should be one and one-half times the intensity of the *fill*. Although this rule can be used as a guide, such things as the studio's ceiling height, the distance from the lighting instruments to the subject, reflectance of the subject's clothing and skin, type of television camera equipment used, and the degree of contrast with the background, must be considered when adjusting intensity.

To test your newly acquired skills, light a live subject in the television studio keeping in mind the rules for correct intensity adjustment. Have your lighting director or instructor evaluate your work.

Checklist For Intensity Adjustment of The Back Light

1. The function of the *back* light is to separate the subject from the background by rimming the hair and shoulders, thus bringing out the modeling or three-dimensional qualities of that subject.
2. Too much *back* light intensity will cause the subject to overly dominate the scene in addition to producing an annoying halo effect around the subject's head.
3. Too little *back* light intensity may be detected when the subject appears to blend into the background.
4. Under *ideal* conditions the *back* light should be equal to one and one-half times the intensity of the *key* light.

Checklist For Intensity Adjustment of The Fill Light

1. The *fill* light is a supplementary form of illumination used to *reduce* the shadow cast by the *key* light.
2. Too much *fill* light intensity will diminish the modeling effect produced by the *key* light. This effect may be especially noted on the cheeks, nose, and above the eyes.
3. Too little *fill* light intensity may be noted by an extreme contrast between the *key* and *fill*. The *key* will overly dominate the scene.
4. Under *ideal* conditions, the *fill* light should be equal to two-thirds the intensity of the *key* light.

Checklist For Intensity Adjustment of The Key Light

1. The *key* is the principal source of illumination and should illuminate three-fourths of the subject's face.
2. Too much *key* light intensity will cause extreme contrast on the subject's face.
3. Too little *key* light intensity may be detected by: a shadow cast on both sides of the subject's nose, a shadow cast on the right side of the subject's face, and an apparent recessing of the subject's features.
4. Under ideal conditions, the *key* should be one and one-half times the intensity of the *fill*.

Chapter 3
Multiple or Moving Cameras

The previous two chapters should have provided you with enough information to achieve correct positioning and intensity adjustment of the *key, back,* and *fill* lights. Figure 3-1 illustrates the effect. Because this basic three-light setup is appropriate only when the camera and subject remain in a stationary position, we will now consider a lighting setup which enables us to have a movable subject and a movable camera.

STATIONARY CAMERA SETUP

Before illustrating this new lighting arrangement, let's quickly review the main points covered in our basic three-light activity. The *key* light is the principal source of illumination and is generally considered to be the most important light in

Fig. 3-1. Key, back, fill lights correct.

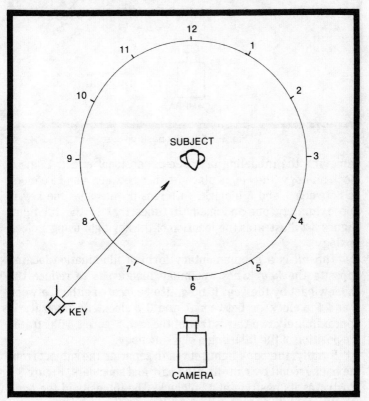

Fig. 3-2. Key light position.

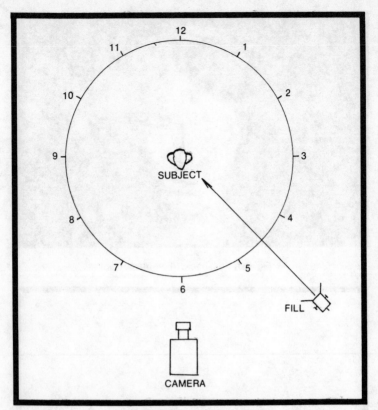

Fig. 3-3. Fill light position.

achieving the modeling or three-dimensional effect. Using a clock analogy, the *key* is placed either between 4 and 5 o'clock or between 7 and 8 o'clock. In terms of intensity, the key is approximately one-and-one-half times that of the fill light. Figure 3-2 illustrates the location of the key light using a clock analogy.

The *fill* is a supplementary form of illumination located opposite the *key*, whose primary function is to reduce the shadow cast by the *key*. It may also be located either between 4 and 5 o'clock or between 7 and 8 o'clock. Its intensity is approximately two-thirds that of the *key*. Figure 3-3 illustrates the position of the *fill* using a clock analogy.

Finally, the *back* light serves to separate the subject from the background by rimming the hair and shoulders. Figure 3-4 illustrates its position at 12 o'clock. The intensity of the *back* should equal that of the *key* plus *fill*.

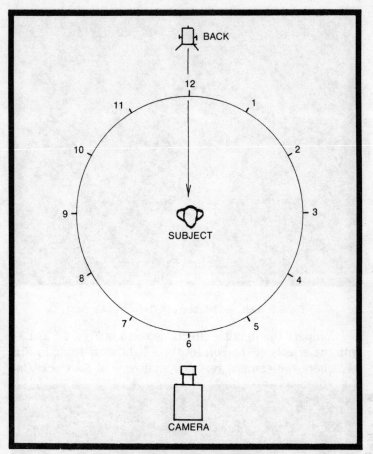

Fig. 3-4. Back light position.

MOVING CAMERA SETUP

We will now attempt to develop a lighting arrangement which will allow a television camera to move on an arc from 4 o'clock to 8 o'clock, while even illumination is maintained across a subject's face as he or she turns to the camera at each point.

Examine Figs. 3-5 and 3-6. Figure 3-5 illustrates the effect of the standard three-light setup with the camera located at 4 o'clock. Notice that the camera right side of the subject's head is in medium-to-dark shadow. Figure 3-6 illustrates the effect of the same three-light setup taken from a camera viewpoint of 8 o'clock. In this instance, the shadow falls on the camera left side of the subject's head.

Fig. 3-5. Back, key, fill correct. Camera at 4 o'clock.

Compare the lighting effects depicted in Figs. 3-5 and 3-6 with the effects of the correct three-light setup found in Fig. 3-1, where the camera remains stationary at 6 o'clock. One

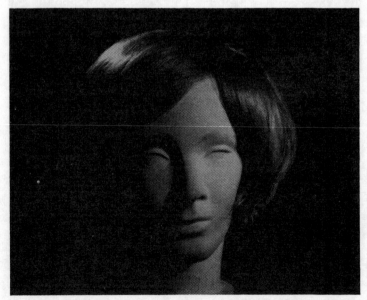

Fig. 3-6. Back, key, fill correct. Camera at 8 o'clock.

basic difference lies in the darkness of the shadow cast by the improper placement of the *fill* light in Figs. 3-5 and 3-6.

Figure 3-7 shows a subject lighted so that the television camera is able to move on an arc from 4 to 8 o'clock and at the same time maintain even illumination across the subject's face. How many lights do you think are needed to achieve such an effect? List the names and number of each light you think is required to achieve this effect.

Draw in the locations of the lighting instruments on the lighting grid and model in Fig. 3-8. Note again that such a diagram allows you to position the lights vertically and horizontally. The grid should be used for horizontal positioning, and the model is to be used for vertical positioning.

Correct lighting of the problem in question requires four lights: A *back*, a *key*, and two *fills*.

The *back* light should be placed at 12 o'clock as it has been in previous setups. In addition, it should be placed at a 45° to 75° vertical angle above a line parallel to the studio floor and passing through the subject's eye. The *back* light's intensity should be equal to that of the *key* plus *fill* lights.

Check your answer to see if you included a *back* light. Also check whether you placed it on the lighting grid at 12 o'clock.

Fig. 3-7. Proper lighting for camera swing from 4 to 8 o'clock.

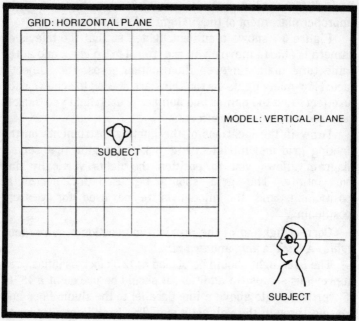

Fig. 3-8. Lighting grid and model.

The *key* light must be placed at 6 o'clock, the midpoint on the swing of the camera's arc. Figure 3-9 depicts a subject shot from the 4 o'clock position with the *key* placed at 6 o'clock.

Fig. 3-9. Back at 12 o'clock, key at 6 o'clock, camera at 4 o'clock.

Notice that from this location the *key* is coming from the camera left side of your picture and performs its modeling function by illuminating approximately three-fourths of the subject's face. One quarter of the subject's face is now in deep shadow.

The same rules of thumb regarding intensity adjustment apply here as they did in the three-light setup. The *key* is one-and-one-half times the intensity of the *fill*, although in this shot, the *fill* has not yet been added. Again check your answer to see if you included a *key* light and if you positioned the *key* at 6 o'clock on the lighting grid.

Figure 3-10 shows a model photographed from the 8 o'clock position with the *key* placed at 6 o'clock. Notice that from this location, the *key* is coming from the right-hand side of the picture, and again performs its modeling function by illuminating approximately three-fourths of the subject's face. We have simply reversed the side on which the *key* appears by changing the direction in which the subject faces, and by placing the camera at a different position. Intensity remains at one-and-one-half times that of the *fill* which has not yet been added in Fig. 3-10.

Fig. 3-10. Key at 6 o'clock, back at 12 o'clock, camera at 8 o'clock.

Fig. 3-11. Key at 6 o'clock, back at 12 o'clock, camera at 4 o'clock, fill at 3 o'clock.

Figure 3-11 shows a subject shot from the 4 o'clock position with a *fill* light added at 3 o'clock. From this location, we approach the same basic *key-fill* combination found in our standard three-light arrangement. The only difference is that the *back* is slightly to the camera right side of your picture with our subject turned to 4 o'clock. This setup focuses the *back* light's rays off to one side of the subject's head. This is one compromise which must be made in using our setup.

Compare Fig. 3-11 with Fig. 3-1 which illustrates a correct three-light arrangement with the camera placed at 6 o'clock. In adjusting the intensity of the *fill*, follow the same rule of thumb as used in the previous three-light activity: The *fill* should be set at two-thirds the intensity of the *key*. Did you include a *fill* in your answer? If so, check your lighting grid to determine if you placed the fill at 3 o'clock.

Figure 3-12 shows an effect achieved when the camera is located at 8 o'clock with our present three lights in operation. Notice that in this arrangement, the right side of the subject's face, or camera left, is unevenly lighted. Remember, the *back* light is located at 12 o'clock, the *key* at 6 o'clock, and the *fill* at 3 o'clock.

Fig. 3-12. Key at 6 o'clock, back at 12 o'clock, fill at 3 o'clock, camera at 8 o'clock.

Fig. 3-13. Camera at 8 o'clock. Four lights in operation. Extra fill added at 9 o'clock.

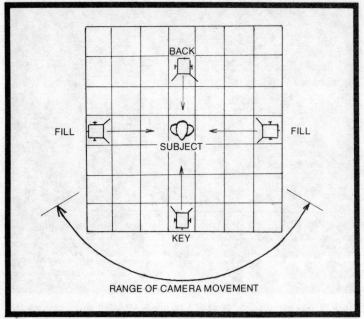

Fig. 3-14. Proper four-light setup.

One light is still missing. Can you determine its location? You want to place a light in a location which will eliminate the shadow cast across the camera left side of the subject's face. The shadow is produced by the *key*, which is currently found at 6 o'clock.

The situation requires a second *fill* light at 9 o'clock. The effect of such placement is illustrated in Fig. 3-13. The camera is located at 8 o'clock in this example. The difference lies in the placement of the *back* light. Positioned at 12 o'clock, the *back* causes more light to fall on the right side of the subject's hair, or on the camera left side of Fig. 3-13.

The same rule of thumb for setting intensity applies: The *fill* should be two-thirds the intensity of the *key*.

Check your answer by referring to the lighting grid you filled out earlier. The correct setup is shown in Fig. 3-14.

Review

Figure 3-15 depicts a subject shot from the 6 o'clock position with all four lights turned on. A *key* is located at 6 o'clock, a *fill* is located at 3 o'clock, a second *fill* is located at 9 o'clock, and a *back* is located at 12 o'clock. The intensity ratios are as follows: The *back* is equal to the *key* plus one *fill*, and each *fill* is two-thirds that of the *key*. Conversely, the *key* is one-and-one-half times the intensity of each *fill*. Again, this is a rule of thumb only.

Intensity may vary according to studio ceiling height, distance of lighting instruments from the subject, type of camera equipment used, the reflectance of the subject's skin and clothing, and the degree of contrast with the background.

Compromises

Before concluding this exercise you should realize that in achieving our four-light movable camera and subject setup, we are making a few compromises in the process.

With the camera located at 8 o'clock and 4 o'clock, we have good modeling from our *key* and *fill* lights; however, our *back* light causes too much side-back illumination, either to the camera left side or camera right side of the subject's head.

Refer to Figs. 3-16 and 3-17 and note these compromises. With the camera placed at 6 o'clock we have a good standard *back* lighting; however, the effect from the *key* and two *fills*

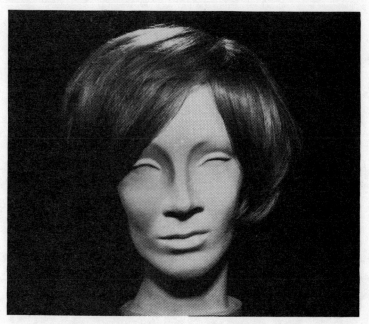

Fig. 3-15. Four-light setup. Camera at 6 o'clock.

Fig. 3-16. Four-light setup. Camera at 8 o'clock.

Fig. 3-17. Four-light setup. Camera at 4 o'clock.

leaves a rather flat-looking picture. Refer again to Fig. 3-15. Compromises such as these are acceptable when movable cameras and subjects are desired.

If you feel confident that you can light a subject to achieve even illumination, thus enabling the camera to move on an arc from an 8 o'clock to a 4 o'clock position, test your newly acquired skills. Light a subject in your television studio employing this four-light arrangement. Have your lighting director or instructor evaluate your performance.

Chapter 4
Multiple Subjects

Chapter Objectives

Given one television camera. multiple spotlights. and multiple subjects located in a television studio. the reader will identify. label. position. and set the intensities of the lighting instruments needed to achieve balanced and equal illumination between subjects photographed from a camera location extending along an arc approximately 120°to 200°on a hypothetical circle.

Chapter 3 demonstrated how to light a subject and maintain even illumination while a camera or cameras moved on an arc from 4 to 8 o'clock. This chapter will examine a lighting system devised to illuminate two or more subjects on a television set. The four-light system used in Chapter 3 will be modified to include additional lighting instruments.

THE SETUP

Figure 4-1 illustrates two subjects illuminated correctly.

As you examine Fig. 4-1, think of a lighting arrangement that will enable you to duplicate the effect. Jot down the number of lighting instruments you feel will be needed and identify the location of each *back, key,* and *fill* light. Draw their locations on the grid in Fig. 4-2 which shows two subjects.

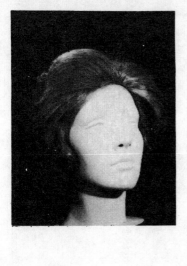
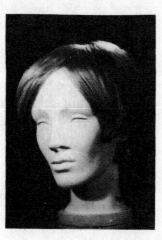

Fig. 4-1. Two subjects with proper back, key, and fill lighting.

The Back Lights

The lighting arrangement used to light the two individuals shown in Fig. 4-1 is very similar to that found in the four-light system described in Chapter 3.

We will begin with the *back* light. You should recall from the previous three chapters that in each single subject setup a

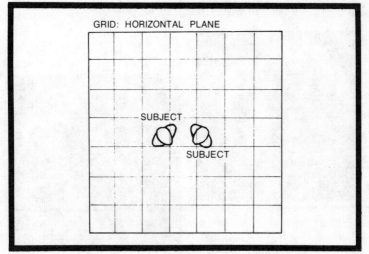

Fig. 4-2. Lighting grid.

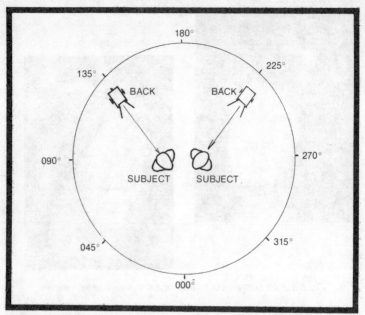

Fig. 4-3. Back lights as degree points on a circle.

back light was used. In the case of multiple subjects, a *back* light is needed for each individual. In the example at hand, two *back* lights are required. They would be placed directly behind each individual. Figure 4-3 shows the positions of the *back* lights as degree points on a circle. The lighting effect which results from such placement is shown in Fig. 4-4.

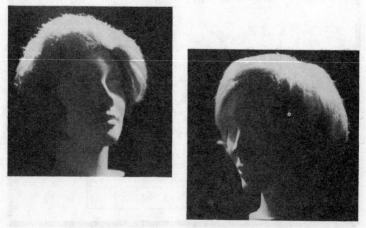

Fig. 4-4. Two subjects lighted by two back lights.

Did you identify a need for two *back* lights in Fig. 4-2 and did you position each *back* in the locations shown in Fig. 4-3?

Subjects more than two feet apart on a set each need a *back* light.

To highlight our point regarding moving and multiple subjects, we have been using Fresnel spotlights which have been adjusted to relatively narrow beam spreads.

The Key Lights

Next we shall consider the *key* lights, their numbers and relative locations. The same rule of thumb used for adding *back* lights applies here: Subjects located at a distance greater than two feet from one another each need a separate *key* light. Because we have two subjects which are separated by more than two feet in our example, we will need two *key* lights. Figure 4-5 shows the correct locations of these two *key* lights.

The resultant lighting effect is shown in Fig. 4-6. Again, we are using Fresnel spots, beamed down to a narrow angle.

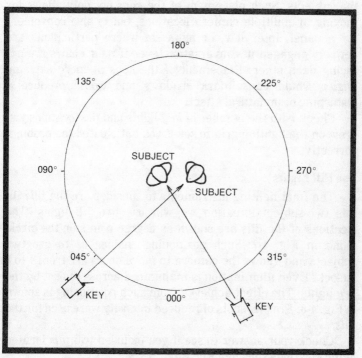

Fig. 4-5. Key lights as degree points on a circle.

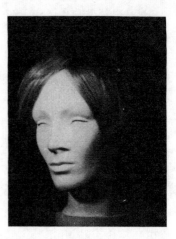

Fig. 4-6. Two subjects lighted by two key lights.

Also note that both *key* lights are placed directly in front of the subjects. Such placement of the *keys* not only allows for moving or multiple camera locations, but is also convenient for a panel, interview, or news set where participants are actively engaged in conversation, even if their chairs are not facing each other. Placement of the *keys* at more extreme angles would cause dark shadows and would produce a disturbing or unnatural effect.

Check both the number of *key* lights and the locations you drew on the lighting grid to see if you anticipated the problem correctly.

The Fill Lights

The final lighting instruments to consider are the *fills*. In this two-subject situation we will use two *fill* lights. The locations of the *fills* are shown as degree points on the circle found in Fig. 4-7. Such positioning enables us to use two subjects and allows the camera to move on an arc from 4 to 8 o'clock. Even illumination is maintained across the set by the *key* lights. The effect achieved from such positioning is shown in Fig. 4-8. Fresnel spots of reduced intensity were used for the *fills*.

Check your answer to see if you included two *fills* located at the positions shown in Fig. 4-7.

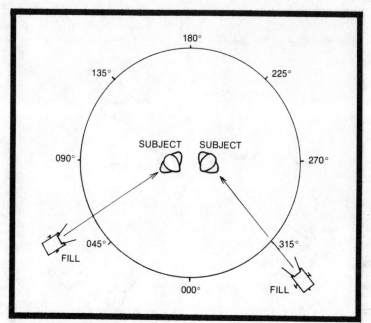

Fig. 4-7. Fill lights as degree points on a circle.

Compromises

The six-light arrangement just described brings with it a few compromises. Basically, the modeling effect which characterized the three-light, single-subject arrangement is

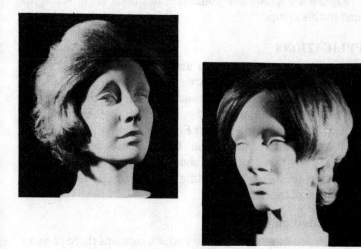

Fig. 4-8. Two subjects lighted by two fill lights.

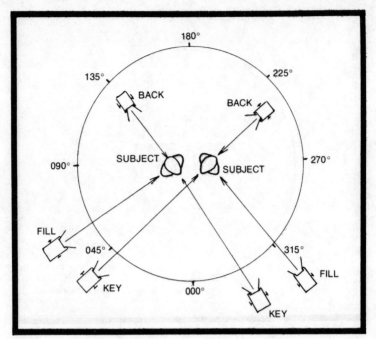

Fig. 4-9. Six-light setup for two subjects.

diminished. The resulting picture displays a flat appearance, and a shadowless condition begins to emerge. Note this condition by re-examining Fig. 4-1.

Figure 4-9 shows the combined locations of all six lights found in this setup.

APPLICATIONS

Now we'll turn briefly to an application of the six-light system. Figure 4-10 shows three subjects, one seated on the camera left side of the picture and two seated on the right side.

Think about the similarities in seating between subjects found in Fig. 4-10 and those in Fig. 4-9. Label the positions of the lighting instruments you think would be needed to illuminate the three subjects shown in Fig. 4-10. In sketching the lighting setup, use the lighting grid in Fig. 4-11 which shows the location of three subjects.

Lighting Multiple Areas

When you begin to light a set which contains three or more subjects, it is generally possible to utilize principles found in a

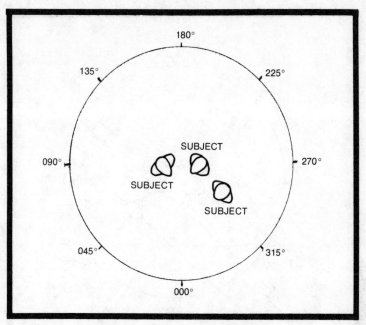

Fig. 4-10. Three subjects on a set.

simple one- or two-man set. The number of lights and their specific locations will depend upon the positions of the subjects, distances from one another, the range of camera movement desired, and the number of subjects involved.

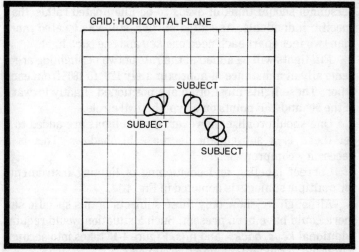

Fig. 4-11. Lighting grid.

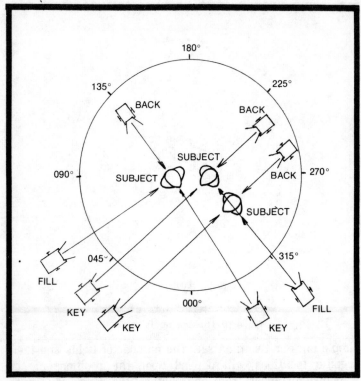

Fig. 4-12. Correct lighting for three subjects.

In addition, when dealing with multiple subjects, lighting personnel should think of *areas* to be illuminated rather than specific individuals. As stated earlier, subjects located more than two feet apart each need one *key* and one *back* light.

Fill lights will be added at the rate of two per lighting area, generally at a distance of approximately 120° to 180° from each other. These lights most often are positioned slightly forward of the 90° and 270° points on a hypothetical circle.

One should realize, however, that as lights are added to a set there is a subsequent decrease in shadows. This is a necessary compromise.

Correct labeling and positioning of lighting instruments for multiple subjects is depicted in Fig. 4-12.

Although we show only three subjects in this specific set, more could have been present. Such a situation would require additional *keys*, *backs*, and *fills*. Figure 4-13 takes into account a lighting arrangement with five subjects.

Focusing Attention

Light has a profound influence on focusing attention toward or away from specific subjects at given points in time. The amount of light added to a set determines whether a television director can take advantage of the full depth-of-field capability of his camera's lens. In an interview or news set where two or more individuals demand equal importance, all should have equal illumination. Equality of illumination enables a television cameraman to place one subject in focus in the foreground, while keeping the background out of focus. A simple rolling of the camera's focus knob will also enable the foreground subject to go out of focus while a subject located in the background suddenly appears in focus. Figure 4-14 shows the influence of proper lighting on depth-of-field.

Figure 4-15 shows a foreground subject in focus with a background subject remaining out of focus. Figure 4-16 reverses this process. Here the foreground subject is out of focus, while the background subject is in focus.

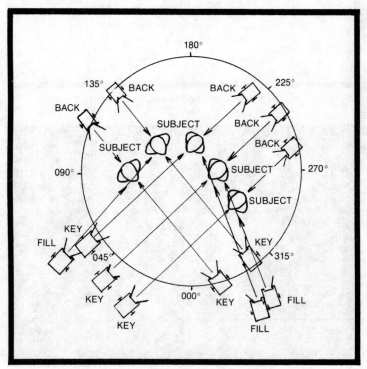

Fig. 4-13. Correct lighting setup for five subjects.

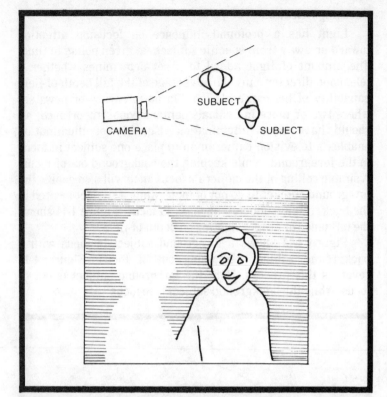

Fig. 4-14. Lighting and depth-of-field.

Fig. 4-15. Foreground subject in focus, background out of focus.

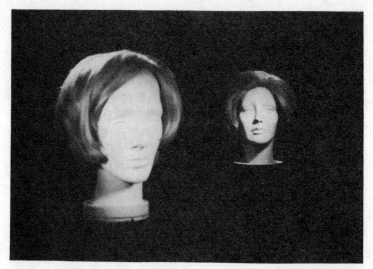

Fig. 4-16. Foreground subject out of focus, background subject in focus.

Providing Dramatic Appeal

Finally, lighting two or more subjects in a way that is out of balance may produce an effect such as that shown in Fig. 4-17. This effect, although disturbing for an interview or news format, lends itself well to a theatrical format. The extreme

Fig. 4-17. Subjects illuminated in a way that is out of balance.

contrast between subject and set, or subject and another subject, brings with it a dramatic appeal often quite desirable in a theatrical production.

Proper lighting intensity is, of course, only one element affecting depth-of-field. Of equal importance is the focal length of a lens, the f-stop adjustment which is related to the amount of light present, and the distance between a subject and the camera. A large diaphragm opening (set by a small f-stop number) will decrease the depth-of-field. A small diaphragm opening (set by a large f-stop number) will increase depth-of-field.

SUMMARY

You have seen how to properly light multiple subjects within a television set. To summarize:

A modified version of a simple four-light arrangement is used to light two or more subjects. Subjects located more than two feet from one another each need a *key* and *back* light. Two *fill* lights are generally used at extreme angles slightly in front of the 90° and 270° points on a hypothetical circle for each lighting *area* used.

Intensity ratios are the same as those found in the basic three-light arrangements: Each *back* should be equal in intensity to one *key* plus one *fill*. Each *key* should be one-and-one half times the intensity of each *fill*.

Finally, depth-of-field considerations enter into the lighting of multiple subjects. In those instances where straightforward news reporting, interview, or panel discussion formats exist, it is important that each subject receive equal and even illumination. The even illumination makes it possible for a director to gain the full advantage of the depth-of-field capability of each camera lens used. For dramatic flavor, however, it is often advantageous to provide extreme contrasts in lighting between the subjects and the set or among the subjects themselves.

Take your new knowledge into the television studio and light two or more subjects using the lighting principles described in this chapter.

Chapter 5
Color

Chapter 5

Color

Chapter Objectives

The reader will acquire a practical working knowledge of the specific requirements of the image-orthicon/vidicon. Plumbicon. and single-tube vidicon color cameras. and will be able to select and manipulate studio production techniques appropriate to each. The reader will be able to identify and solve problems of color television production associated with base illumination. color temperature. and contrast range found in broadcast and closed-circuit systems.

A book dealing with television lighting would be deficient if it did not attempt to tackle the problem of lighting for color. Chapter 5 deals with quality and intensity requirements for broadcast and closed-circuit color television equipment. Intensity is produced by base illumination, and quality is dependent upon color temperature, a term used to describe the degree of whiteness of a light source.

Most problems associated with lighting for color television are generated during periods of transition from a black-and-white to a color system. A complete and modern color system, designed from the ground up, poses few problems beyond its initial expense.

A hybrid system, composed of bits and pieces from black-and-white television, a number of photofloods or backup lights from a local theatre group, and a mail-order color camera complete with accessories, will create numerous problems. Its various elements will not be matched in several important respects: The provision of the necessary base illumination, the maintenance of an appropriate contrast range involving the interaction between the amount of light provided and the reflectance value of the object to be televised, and adherence to the proper color temperature standards. Equipment is not matched and is not a part of a unified system, unless performance standards are shared in all of these areas.

THE CAMERA

The critical element to consider when selecting items for color television production is the camera. Each type of color camera has its own set of performance characteristics or requirements. Failure to meet any one of these requirements will result in the reproduction of a picture of inferior quality.

The major differences between the various color cameras now in use lies in their internal construction. Basically, cameras will be fitted with either image-orthicon, vidicon, or Plumbicon pickup tubes. Illumination requirements vary from 150 footcandles to 800 footcandles. The contrast range within the picture varies from 10:1 to 30:1, the latter providing a rich picture with many subtle tints, shades, and degrees of brightness. Failure to provide light of the proper color temperature destroys whatever color fidelity the cameras were designed to produce. This effect is shown in Fig. 5-1. (This and all other color photographs appear in the front of the book.)

The characteristics of a camera are important to consider when determining the color an object is to be painted, the lighting instruments and intensities to be used, the degree of contrast between highlights and shadows, and the distance between the camera and the object. Overlooking these factors may create a picture that, at best, will be "noisy." This means it will display electronic disturbance in the form of "snow," which dominates the darker areas. More probably, the picture will be beyond adjustment until the offending factor is corrected. The problem of picture noise is shown in Fig. 5-2. (See front of book.)

Image-Orthicon/Vidicon Camera

The first color cameras that dominated production at the national level contain one image-orthicon and three vidicon pickup tubes. These have now been relegated to second-line status. In these cameras, the light reflected from the scene being televised passes through the camera lens and splits. One portion of the light is directed to the image-orthicon tube which provides a black-and-white luminance signal designed to make the final product look sharp and well-defined. The other portion of the light entering the camera becomes the chrominance signal. It is again split by a series of mirrors into three parts. Each part is directed to one of the vidicon tubes.

Before the light bearing the image of the scene can reach a vidicon tube, it must pass through a red, green, or blue color filter. These colors represent the primary colors of light. All other colors can be mixed from these three colors, which is exactly what happens,in a pointillist way, on the face of the picture tube in the television receiver.

Because the light is split so many ways and because it must pass through relatively dense color filters, an extreme amount of light must be reflected from the scene if this type of camera is to function properly. Figure 5-3 helps to clarify the procedure by which light entering the lens of this camera splits, and activates the four pickup tubes. Figure 5-4 depicts the quality of picture which is characteristic of a combination image-orthicon/vidicon tube color camera. (See front of book.)

Two factors govern the amount of light reflected by a television scene: The amount of light focused on the scene, and the colors of the objects located within the scene. Generally, no colors darker than a middle gray are used with the

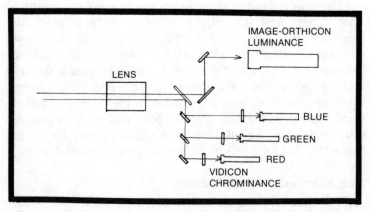

Fig. 5-3. Light splits upon entering the image-orthicon/vidicon camera.

image-orthicon/vidicon type color camera. This color selection, plus about 800 footcandles of light and special attention to the elimination of shadow areas, will create the right conditions for a good picture.

The elimination of shadows in scenes covered by this type of camera is necessary because the camera cannot tolerate a contrast ratio greater than 15:1 without producing a noisy picture. Extra *fill* lights must be used to eliminate the darker shadows.

The provision of 800 footcandles of light from the *key* and *fill* positions creates an extreme amount of heat in the studio. This places a strain on the studio cooling system and on those who perform under the lights. Even in relatively brief sessions (two hours or less), desk tops become hot to the touch, and flowers wilt. Objects painted black can absorb enough light energy to startle the performer handling them and to destroy many demonstrations and experiments.

In using this camera it is therefore necessary that lighting positions and intensities be established well before the actual production time so that the air and objects within the scene will have had time to cool before filming begins.

Plumbicon Camera

The camera system which replaced the image-orthicon/vidicon variety as the national standard in commercial and public broadcasting is built around three Plumbicon type pickup tubes—one for each of the primary colors of light. This system represents a decade of technical improvement over the earlier camera and provides better pictures under reduced light levels.

Specifically, the camera operates under fewer than 200 footcandles of light and can accommodate a 30:1 range of light-dark contrasts. Pictures can feature deep shadows, dark reds, blues, greens, and browns, and the modeling effect of the *key* light can be maintained.

This *key* light modeling was difficult to achieve in the 800 footcandle environment because there was so much light from so many different directions. The chiaroscuro effect that enhanced the texture of human skin and the shape of the head was therefore lost. A representative picture of the Plumbicon type camera can be seen in Fig. 5-5. (See front of book.)

Another technical characteristic of the Plumbicon system deserves consideration by the lighting designer. Extremely bright highlights, such as reflections on metal or glass, will appear as white holes in the picture. This condition exists because the camera system cannot produce a range of color from deep shadow areas through bright highlights without distorting something in the picture. The metallic highlights are therefore sacrificed and lost in the processing.

Technically, this condition is caused by the fact that the camera's *peak limiting exposure curve*, an expression of electronic capacity, remains even. That means the camera reaches a processing barrier all at once, rather than gradually or with some warning. A typical warning given by other cameras might be a color distortion appearing before the picture was lost at the point of the bright or super energized reflection. Figure 5-6, in the front of the book, illustrates the problem of white holes.

While the elimination of all such reflection is impractical, steps can be taken to reduce it in broad areas. Can you think of a procedure for counteracting this problem?

The answer is to avoid placing the lights in such a way that a mirror-like reflection from flat surfaces in the scene finds its way to the camera. This potential problem introduces another reason for knowing where the cameras will be placed before arranging the lighting instruments. Figure 5-7 shows a proper light plot for counteracting the reflectance problem.

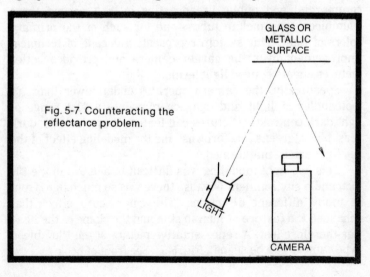

Fig. 5-7. Counteracting the reflectance problem.

Small and very thin lines of extremely bright reflection, as on the edges of eyeglasses, may actually enhance the picture by adding sparkle to it. This effect can boomerang when the subject turns his head so that light from a specific lighting instrument is reflected directly into a camera. When this happens, the whole eyeglass lens becomes a white hole. In the course of acting, a performer may turn his head from side to side or tilt it up and down. The lighting designer must apply the *key* and *fill* plan in relation to a specific camera position keeping all lights at a relatively high angle. This arrangement will reduce the chance that a massive reflection will be created by the eyeglasses.

Single-Tube Vidicon Camera

A third color camera system in wide usage today is the single-tube vidicon variety. In this system, the three color filters are rotated past the vidicon pickup tube and the three color circuits operate in sequence rather than simultaneously. To reduce the "lag" or "smear," which is a picture distortion charactersitic of vidicon tubes, the camera must be supplied with approximately 300 footcandles of light. An acceptable still picture can be produced with less light if a very low contrast range of 10:1 is maintained. Video noise will be created if a greater contrast range is supplied. A comet-like tail will appear in association with any highlights on objects that move or that are covered by a moving camera. This effect is not illustrated here because it can result in damage to the tube.

The quality of the picture produced by these relatively inexpensive single-tube vidicon cameras is appropriate to closed-circuit use. The picture appears best when presented directly on the television receiver as shown in Fig. 5-8, in the front of the book.

The quality loss is often noticeable when the video signal is recorded and then replayed on a videotape recorder. The electronic signal produced is just not accurate enough to withstand multiple recording, transmission, and broadcast operations.

The cameras are inexpensive, conducive to being held by hand, and simple to operate, all of which makes them popular for instructional purposes. However, greater care must be exercised in the control of the scenic elements to be televised by these cameras than with the broadcast cameras previously described.

BASE ILLUMINATION

Much has been written about the base illumination requirements of color television. There is a temptation to fill the studio with floodlights and turn them all on as a means of providing an even illumination throughout the studio. This is not the approach to take if you expect to create an attractive picture which enhances your program and allows the performers to appear as personable characters.

At the very least, *key* and *back* lights can be placed in the traditional positions while floodlights can be used to *fill* the resulting shadow areas. Care must be taken to reduce the amount of contrast between the highlights created by the *key* and the shadows filled by the floods to the point where no noise appears in the shadow or fill areas. While the picture will not appear as sharp as the best black-and-white image, some modeling effect will be evident, and the picture will not seem flat.

The background areas can be illuminated evenly with floodlights. This background should be less bright than the objects in the acting area. The fact that the area is a greater

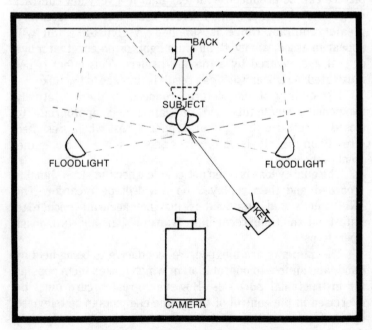

Fig. 5-9. Floodlights illuminate background.

distance from the camera helps keep the brightness down and care can be taken to illuminate it less intensely. Figure 5-9 clarifies such a lighting arrangement.

The differences allowed between highlight and shadow areas for a 10:1 contrast range camera system are going to be small. The 15:1 camera is capable of producing a more varied picture although the pastel tints will still predominate. The film industry has led audiences to expect the highest pictorial standards as a matter of course. An effective contrast range of up to 160:1 is possible in film, while the best television can expect to achieve is about 30:1.

Several factors are involved in this contrast range comparison. First, film is viewed in darkness; television is generally viewed in an illuminated room. This difference in viewing situation causes television pictures to seem paler than film pictures.

Second, both the tonal contrast within the scene and the intensity contrast within the lighting itself influence the general contrast range within the picture. The inter-relationship between these two variables dictates that the greater the tonal contrast within the scene, the less the contrast that can be allowed in the lighting. Theoretically, scenery could be painted to look perfectly natural anywhere within this scale. The human face, however, provides a problem. Its normal tonal range is not great in areas other than the eyes and mouth. Therefore, the use of modeling light is critical to the representation of its three-dimensional quality. The different levels of brightness on the skin areas of the face will be created by the angle of the skin to the camera and the angle and intensity of the *key, fill,* and *back* lights.

COLOR TEMPERATURE

It may seem that the easiest way to adjust the total contrast range is with lighting dimmers. In black-and-white television, dimmers are used for this purpose. The designer can save time by visually checking the intensity adjustments on a television monitor as they are made. If this is not possible, the designer can estimate the intensity ratio with the help of a light meter.

In color television, however, dimmers are not used with lighting instruments focused on the performers because the skin tones would appear unnatural. This happens because dimming the instruments acts to change the *color temperature* of the light by reducing the electrical power to that light. Refer once again to Fig. 5-1, which illustrates this problem.

Color temperature, which describes the degree of whiteness of a light source, is expressed in "degrees Kelvin" (e.g., 3200° K). The number indicates a relationship to the temperature of the filament in an incandescent light. The hotter the filament gets, the whiter it glows, and the whiter the light that is produced. Conversely, if the filament is heated to a relatively low temperature, it carries a lower Kelvin rating (e.g., 2500° K) and produces a reddish-yellow light.

This is important because a red light does not contain green frequencies and, therefore, cannot be used to illuminate a green object. Perfectly white light contains all of the spectral frequencies and can be used to illuminate all colors without distortion. Since there are many problems involved with filming for color television, it behooves us to avoid distortion problems caused by colored light.

The degree of whiteness which has become an industry standard is rated at 3200° K. Some lighting instruments are designed to produce it, and equipment is generally calibrated to function at that level.

Dimmers are used in color television to adjust the intensity of the light on background areas. Color distortion in scenery will not be noticed as long as skin tones look natural. But if dimmers are placed on background areas, they can save a lot of time in the adjustment of the contrast range throughout the entire scene.

SPECIAL PROBLEMS

Quartz-iodine lamps are preferred for color television over the standard tungsten filament lamps because a whiter light can be created over a longer operating life with about one-third the electrical power. Unlike tungsten, which glows redder with age, the filament in the quartz lamp glows at a constant degree of whiteness throughout its life. It will not glow white if the power to it is reduced by a dimmer, however. With reduced power, it will act like any tungsten filament and glow yellow or red.

Mixed Equipment

Because lighting equipment is expensive, it is not unusual for a studio to acquire the quartz-iodine instruments gradually. This forces a combination of instrument types for ambitious projects that arise during the period of transition from black-and-white to color.

If tungsten and quartz instruments must be mixed, it is best to illuminate the performers with quartz and the background areas with tungsten. In this way. the skin tones will remain controlled and whatever distortion is created by the tungsten will be limited to the background, where it will be the least noticeable.

It may not be possible to separate the instruments in this manner and, if a combination is unavoidable, care must be taken to maintain the same lighting balance throughout the scene from each camera position. This is a very difficult task. Failure to achieve the lighting balance will result in highlights on performers' faces which can range from orange to blue depending upon the instrument and camera positions. While some electronic adjustment of the color is possible for a given camera in a static position, it is generally considered impossible to maintain such an adjustment for multiple cameras and positions during the course of a program.

Sunlight

These lighting problems will not exist if all instruments in the studio are equipped with the quartz-iodine type lamps. However. problems will exist in production situations outside of the studio which even quartz will not solve.

Sunlight. which is rated from 6500° K to 12,000° K depending upon atmospheric and environmental conditions. can cause an imbalance in color temperature between *key* and *fill* light on the performer's face.

Available incandescent, quartz, mercury-vapor, or fluorescent lamps will not match the existing sunlight, and distortions in highlight and shadow areas will occur in the form of distracting color shifts. In some conditions, powerful arc lights can be used to key exterior scenes.

Problems can be minimized by using reflectors instead of electric lights. Reflectors would insure that the color temperature provided by the sun would be used throughout the scene.

Zoom Lens

Lighting designers, television directors, and engineers must all realize that some change in color values may be inevitable during normal production. The use of a zoom lens to present first a wide view of a scene and then an extreme closeup of the face of one of the performers may involve severe differences in contrast range. A small figure seen in silhouette in front of a sky cyclorama in the widest shot will probably contain a greater range of brightness contrast than will a closeup of the face which obscures almost all of the cyclorama.

Figure 5-10 shows a given contrast range found in a wide shot utilizing a zoom lens. Figure 5-11 illustrates a different contrast range created by an extreme closeup using the same camera zoom lens. (Both Figures appear in front of book.)

For technical reasons, the aesthetic impact of such techniques is often traded for greater control of color values. The performers in such scenes are often illuminated more brightly than normal to reduce the contrasts. This procedure sacrifices some modeling, however.

LIGHTING SETUPS

Most lighting for color television uses extensions of the three-light and four-light systems already presented in this book.

For a program using a stationary camera and subject, the three-light system should be used as a starting point. The *back*, *fill*, and *key* lights should be placed in their standard positions. Floodlights can be arranged to illuminate the background. Their number and overlap will be determined by the intensity desired.

If three-dimensional objects are present in the background, they should be accented with the addition of a special *key* light which parallels the *key* focused on the performer. Generally. a 1.000-watt *key* will be used on the performer, although this may be modified by the distance the *key* is positioned from the performer. The intensity of the *back* and *fill* lights should increase proportionally. As the level of illumination is increased, the amount of ambient, or uncontrolled light, is also increased. This increase in the general level of illumination results in a loss of modeling. Figure 5-12 shows the lighting setup that produced it.

If several camera positions are planned, or if several views of the same acting area are required, a four-light system must be employed. Diagram a lighting plot you think would be

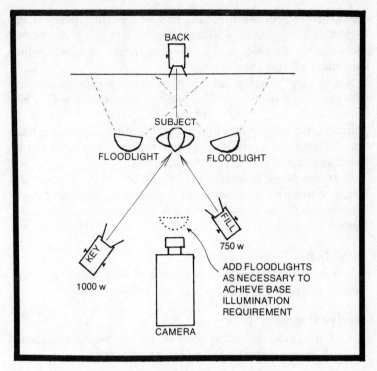

Fig. 5-12. Three-light setup for color shots.

appropriate for multiple camera positions. Don't forget to provide adequate illumination for the background areas.

The *key* should be placed at the 6 o'clock position. Again, an instrument or combination of instruments producing 1,000 watts will be required. The *fill* light must be evenly applied at least 90° on each side of the subject or performer. The background should be treated, as before, with a series of evenly-spaced floodlights. The intensity of the *fill* and background lights should be adjusted to meet the contrast requirements of the cameras being used. Figure 5-13 depicts the proper setup.

Most color camera systems cannot accommodate a high contrast level. If a high contrast between *key* and *fill* is created, the camera will adjust to the *key* and the area illuminated by the *fill* will appear very dark and noisy.

The combination of a relatively bright *fill*, background lights, and frontal *key* produces a comparatively flat picture when the camera is in the 6 o'clock position. The color will

111

compensate somewhat for the lack of modeling effect of the lighting. This plan will provide for camera usage anywhere between the 4 o'clock and 8 o'clock positions, without creating too many contrast problems.

The most modern color cameras have a greater contrast tolerance and more attention is given to modeling with a *key* from an oblique, rather than frontal, position. Backgrounds can be separated more from the acting areas and darker hues can be used. As a result, a greater range of programs can be produced effectively in television studios.

At this point, it seems that the use of film for dramas and other complex programs may give way to videotape—especially if the costs of videotape become equivalent or lower.

SUMMARY

Because this chapter has dealt with specialized material, review questions have been provided below.

Review Questions

1. List the principal causes for problems commonly associated with hybrid color television systems.

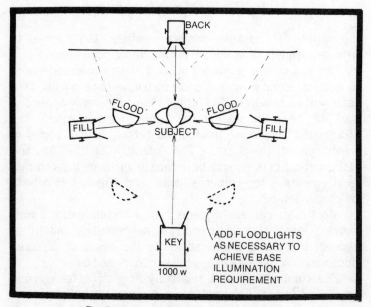

Fig. 5-13. Four-light setup for color shots.

2. List the three most common types of color television cameras used by the commercial industry and closed-circuit operations today.

3. Contrast range for these three varieties of cameras runs from _____ to _____.

4. Video noise often results when a number of important considerations are neglected. List these various considerations.

5. Match the camera characteristics found in Column A with the camera types found in Column B.

Column A	Column B
_____ a. 30:1 contrast range	1. I-O/Vidicon
_____ b. operates under 200 footcandles	2. Plumbicon
_____ c. 10:1 contrast range	3. Vidicon (single-tube)
_____ d. requires 300 footcandles	
_____ e. has four pickup tubes	
_____ f. 15:1 contrast range	
_____ g. requires approximately 800 footcandles	
_____ h. can adjust to strong contrasting colors	

6. Examine the problem depicted in Figure 5-6. Determine what problem is illustrated and diagram a lighting plot which should eliminate such a problem.

7. Figure 5-2 illustrates the problem of video noise as found in an image-orthicon/vidicon system. List the cause of this problem and its solution.

8. Explain the correct procedure for providing adequate base illumination in lighting a set for color television.

9. Dimmers are not recommended for adjusting contrast range in instances where human subjects are involved because the _____ _____ would be adversely affected, thus resulting in unnatural skin tones.

10. When mixing lighting instruments of the quartz-iodine and standard tungsten filament varieties, only the _____ lamps should be used in relation to the acting areas. This is because_____.

Answers

The answers to the review questions are as follows:

1. Problems associated with hybrid color television systems stem from a failure on the part of the various units making up the system to be matched in:

   a. The provision of the necessary base illumination.
   b. The maintenance of an adequate contrast range involving interaction between available light and the reflectance value of the object to be televised.
   c. Adherence to the proper color temperature standards.

2.
   a. Image-orthicon/vidicon
   b. Plumbicon
   c. Vidicon (single-tube)

3. 10:1 to 30:1

4.
   a. Failure to determine the proper color an object is to be painted.
   b. Failure to select the appropriate lighting instruments.
   c. Failure to adjust the correct intensities of each lighting instrument.
   d. Failure to account for the appropriate degree of contrast between highlights and shadows which can be tolerated.
   e. Failure to take into consideration the distance the camera will be from the subject.

5. a. 2: b. 2: c. 3: d. 3: e. 1: f. 1: g. 1: h. 2.

6. Figure 5-6 depicts the problem of extreme reflections which appear as white holes in the picture. Figure 5-7 shows a lighting plot which should at least reduce such a problem.

7. The video noise, appearing in Fig. 5-2, is caused by decreasing the level of illumination found on the subject. To eliminate the problem, one simply needs to increase the level of illumination.

8. *Key* and *back* lights should be placed in their standard locations while floodlights can be employed to fill in

any resulting shadow areas. Special care must be taken to reduce the contrast between the highlights created by the *key* and the shadows filled by the floods, so that virtually little or no noise appears in these fill or shadowy areas. The background should be illuminated evenly with floods and should appear less bright than the acting area.

9. Color temperature
10. Quartz-Iodine. These lamps should be utilized in relation to acting areas since they glow at a constant degree of whiteness throughout their life. Because of this fact, skin tones remain natural in color appearance.

If you feel confident that you have mastered the stated objectives for this chapter, try out some of your newly acquired knowledge in a television studio.

Chapter 6
Graphics

Chapter Objectives

Given a television studio with appropriate lighting instruments. the reader will be able to recognize and solve common problems found in lighting television graphics. and will be able to light graphic materials for television in a manner which serves to clarify and enhance the visual message or special production effects inherent in their construction.

The use of visual or graphic materials in a television program is often essential to the successful transmission of a central theme or message. Without adequate illumination of the graphic material, however, the message is generally lost and the visual material becomes wasted. This chapter will attempt to clarify and focus attention on proper illumination techniques needed in lighting television graphics.

LIGHTING CONSIDERATIONS

A variety of problems must be recognized and solved when lighting graphic materials used in television. First, it must be understood that the term "graphics" may include anything from simple cards bearing white letters on a black background, to glossy photographs or multicolored drawings. It may also include three-dimensional models through which action is seen, onto which the images of characters are

Fig. 6-1. Matte finish graphic.

superimposed, or into which those images are "keyed" or electronically inserted.

Basic Illumination

To light graphics, a basic level of illumination must be provided so that the cameras function properly; then, the reflectivity of the graphic must be considered.

Surface Texture

Surface textures of graphics and props may range from the dullest, least reflective matte finish, as seen in Fig. 6-1, to the highly reflective metal object shown in Fig. 6-2. Some paints and inks will reflect light with mirror-like clarity. Graphic artists often design materials to feature a contrast of textures which depend upon proper lighting for their effect.

Color

The effectiveness of the color contrasts contained in a graphic also depends upon proper lighting. It is important to maintain the desired color values throughout the program by coordinating the illumination of skin, textiles, and painted surfaces so that cameras will not have to be adjusted for each item during a program. Improper lighting can change the apparent color of a person, costume, or graphic.

Lighting Setups

Another factor which requires attention in the lighting of television graphics involves the placement of the lighting

119

instruments in the studio. The size of the graphic and its use within the program often determine patterns of camera movement, which, in turn, determine the placement and lighting of the actors. It is important to keep shadows cast by actors, cameras, and microphone booms away from the graphic materials, and to provide even illumination. This usually eliminates light spilled from the acting areas.

REFLECTANCE PROBLEMS

Several principles apply to the proper lighting of all graphics. The first deals with the reflection and absorption of light energy.

Surface

Glass, certain plastics and enamels, and polished metals *reflect* a high percentage of the light falling upon them. This problem is so severe on spherical or curved surfaces that a dulling spray often must be applied before the object can be displayed effectively on television. Figure 6-3 illustrates high reflection items prior to the application of a dulling spray. A dulling spray has been added in Fig. 6-4. Note the difference between the two pictures.

Flat surfaces which reflect light efficiently can often be placed in the studio in such a way that the light is merely

Fig. 6-2. Highly reflective metal object.

Fig. 6-3. Highly reflective items prior to dulling spray application.

Fig. 6-4. Dulling spray applied to highly reflective items.

reflected away from the camera lens. Take a few moments to think about where you would place a light to avoid reflectance commonly found when lighting graphics with flat surfaces. Refer to Fig. 6-5 after you have formulated your answer.

The example in Fig. 6-5 represents a glossy photograph or shiny record album, which should be lighted from above or to the side and placed in a near vertical position, so that the surface reflection misses the camera. Failure to angle the reflection away from the camera will result in surface glare that obscures the picture or album entirely.

Color

Reflection of light is governed by the color as well as the surface of an object. Would you place greater light intensity on a light or dark-colored object?

In lighting colored graphics, greater illumination is required for the darker materials. Why do you think this is true?

Light colors (white, light yellow, light blue) reflect more light energy than do dark colors (black, dark brown, dark blue). The dark colors absorb much of the light energy. Therefore, a light-colored object will require less light energy, and fewer instruments to illuminate it than will a dark-colored object.

The inclusion of light and dark objects in the same program may require separate lighting treatments so that each object is equally visible on the home television screen.

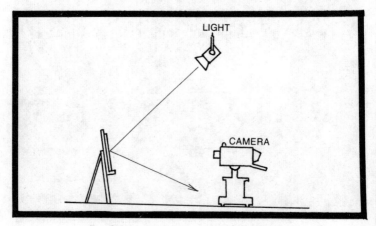

Fig. 6-5. Light placed to avoid reflectance.

Fig. 6-6. Red and blue objects of equal contrast on a gray scale.

Several problems can emerge in the treatment of objects of different color. First, if a red and blue object have the same brightness and reflect the same amount of light, they can appear to be the same color on black-and-white television. Examine Fig. 6-6, which illustrates this problem. The book on the left is blue while the one on the right is red. Color contrasts, so evident in the studio, are often lost in black-and-white television.

If an extreme amount of light energy is focused on a dark object in order to increase its visibility, it may begin to smoke, melt, or even burst into flame. This lends unnecessary excitement to the studio proceedings. It happens because colors absorb that light energy which they do not reflect. Dark colors absorb more than do light colors because they reflect less. The light energy that is absorbed turns into heat, much to the dismay of many a studio crew. Plactic objects are particularly susceptible to damage from too much light.

The amount and quality of the light energy reflected from an object depends upon the color of the object and the amount and quality of the light falling upon it.

Light is a form of electromagnetic radiation and each color represents a different frequency of that radiation. If all frequencies in the visible spectrum are added together, *white* light will result. This *additive* system of color mixing is used to describe the mixture of colors of light.

Pigments, or colors seen as properties of paint, dye, ink, or natural minerals are described by means of a *subtractive* system of color mixing because the mixture of all colors will theoretically result in the creation of a *black* pigment. In theory, a pure white pigment would reflect all frequencies of light energy focused upon it and absorb almost none; a pure black pigment would absorb almost all frequencies of light energy and reflect almost none.

The apparent color of an object, then, is a product of its pigmentation and the quality of the light focused upon it.

A green object will seem to be black if illuminated by a red light because there are no green frequencies in red light to be reflected. Actually, a green pigment is termed "green" because it absorbs all frequencies except green, which it reflects.

This problem arises in the studio when incandescent lights are controlled by dimmers. As the light is dimmed, or turned down, the temperature of the filament in the lamp is reduced; instead of glowing white hot it descends toward only being red hot. The illumination thus produced is short on blue and green. Frequencies and objects on which such light is focused have a reduced capacity to reflect blue and green.

This characteristic of dimmers is often acceptable in the theatre where the human eye views the scene directly; it can, however, cause serious problems in television where the picture must be processed through a relatively narrow electronic window with very limited capacity to handle contrasts in light quality or intensity.

Intensity

The intensity of the light reflected from an object is affected by the colors involved, and the intensity of the reflected light is the key to the adjustment of the cameras. It is important, sometimes imperative, that the lighting within a program be within a narrow range of intensities. A graphic that is too bright or too dim will fail to achieve its purpose and can actually distract the viewer.

Fig. 6-7. Effect of uneven illumination upon a camera card.

List a number of considerations you feel a lighting director should be concerned with in lighting television graphics. Be sure to include ways in which light intensity may be controlled.

Lighting in television, whether it is the product of incandescent or quartz instruments, is best created through the use of an even quality of light throughout the program. If the quality of light is constant, everyone in the studio, from graphic artists to television engineers, can operate from the same base.

The intensity of the light can be controlled by changing the distance between the lighting instrument and the object, by changing the size of the lighting instrument, or by using dimmers. Dimmers provide speed in the adjustment of light, and are invaluable as long as care is taken not to change the quality of light falling upon the central object in a given scene.

SHADOW PROBLEMS

Care must also be taken to illuminate graphics, especially title cards or charts, evenly. What appears to the eye to be relatively even illumination can appear quite uneven to the television camera.

Flat Graphics

In the lighting of flat graphics, even illumination is most important. The result of an unevenly lit graphic can be seen in Fig. 6-7. If you were asked to light a flat graphic for television, where would you place a light to achieve even illumination? Diagram such a setup, positioning the light or lights in their correct locations.

The best way to illuminate such graphics is often with two instruments, one placed at each side and above at about 45° from the horizontal. If light strikes the surface of the graphic at too shallow an angle, it will begin to reveal the surface irregularities and construction details (wrinkled paper, depressed printing, etc.) or the graphic. Refer to Fig. 6-8. Light striking at too shallow an angle can even begin to accentuate a soft or porous surface texture of the paper or cardboard bearing the graphic

The optimum position for a light would seem to be one perpendicular to the graphic, since that could cast no shadows. However, such a position would tend to reflect light from a shiny or hard surface right back into the camera, which should

Fig. 6-8. Effect of light striking visual at too shallow an angle.

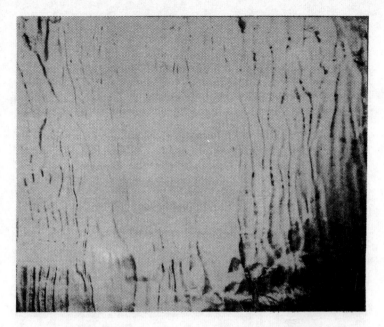

Fig. 6-9. Effect of perpendicular positioning of lights.

be in a position perpendicular to the graphic to avoid a lens distortion. The reflection error is shown in Fig. 6-9.

A lighting instrument placed on this perpendicular centerline behind the camera would also tend to cast the shadow of the camera on the graphic as seen in Fig. 6-10. A light placed on the camera avoids the shadow problem but often reflects right into the lens from a hard-surfaced graphic.

To avoid shadows, place two instruments somewhat as you would two *key* lights of equal intensity, one to the right and one to the left of the graphic as shown in Fig. 6-11. The effect of such placement is depicted in Fig. 6-12.

This technique is particularly important in the illumination of glossy photographs. While these surfaces are commonly smooth, they are also curved, which means that light is more likely to be reflected from the surface into the lens. To avoid this, the photograph must be held flat. The most popular technique involves rubber-cementing it to a piece of heavy cardboard.

Textured Surfaces

Photographs or illustrations from magazines create a greater problem in that they are generally printed on glossy

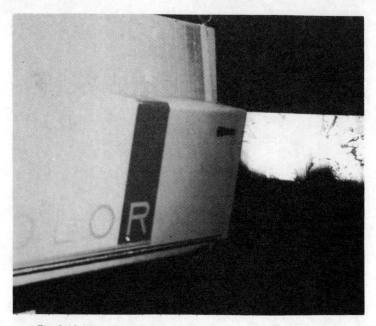

Fig. 6-10. Light placed behind camera casts shadow on graphic.

but thin paper which tears, wrinkles, and stretches easily. Materials of this kind must be cemented to heavy cardboard with great care because they are fragile, and wrinkles are highly reflective and difficult to hide. If you wished to light

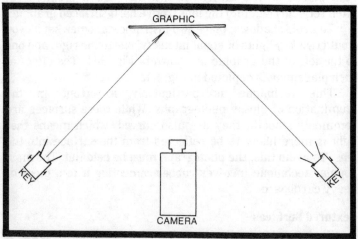

Fig. 6-11. Positioning two key lights.

Fig. 6-12. Graphic correctly illuminated.

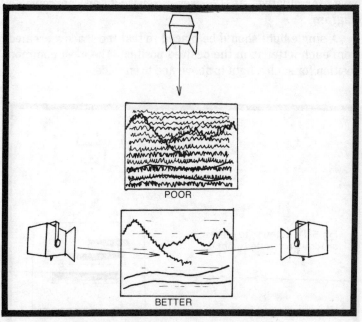

POOR

BETTER

Fig. 6-13. Lighting to hide unsightly wrinkles.

such a graphic to hide the unsightly wrinkles, where would you place the lighting instruments? Diagram such an arrangement, and compare your answer with Fig. 6-13.

Again, the use of two instruments parallel to the wrinkles will often disguise the fact they are present. This principle is basic to the illumination of any textured surface.

The textures of paper, cloth, and plaster are made apparent through the creation of shadows and, to a lesser extent, through the creation of highlights. The hard surfaces of minerals, metals, and plastics are generally revealed through highlights. To create shadows, lights should be focused across the surface depressions; to reduce or eliminate shadows, light should be focused along or parallel to the depressions or ridges. Figure 6-14 shows the location of lights to create shadows. The subsequent result is displayed in Fig. 6-15.

Figure 6-16 depicts a lighting technique for reducing or eliminating shadows by focusing the instruments parallel to a surface depression. The results of this technique are shown in Fig. 6-17.

If the graphic contains raised letters which are to be recognized as being raised, how would you light it? Once you have formulated an answer, construct an appropriate diagram.

A single light should be placed so that the shadow created from each letter is in the desired position. The most common position for such a light is above and to one side.

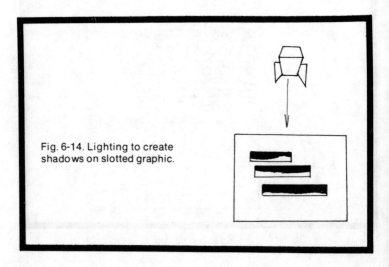

Fig. 6-14. Lighting to create shadows on slotted graphic.

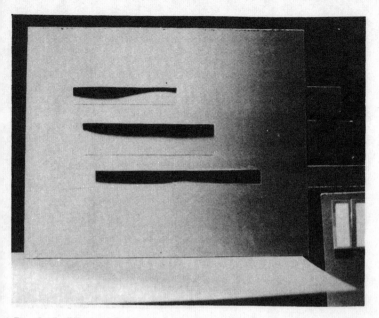

Fig. 6-15. Effect of light focused across surface depression to create shadows on a slotted graphic.

Movement of the light will catch the attention of the viewer and should be designed to contribute something special to the viewer's understanding of the program: A horizontally moving light might indicate the presence of an automobile, a flickering light from below might indicate a campfire. Figure 6-18 shows the conventional setup.

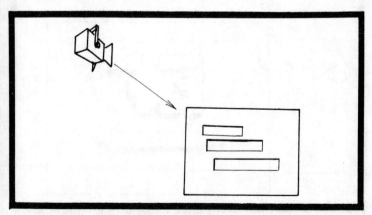

Fig. 6-16. Lighting to eliminate shadows on a slotted graphic.

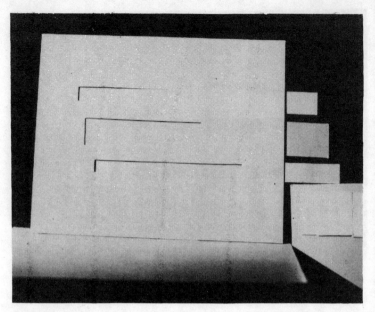

Fig. 6-17. Effect of light focused parallel to surface depressions on a slotted graphic.

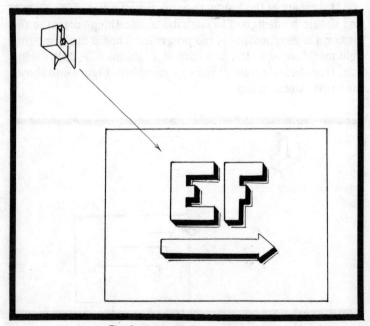

Fig. 6-18. Lighting raised letters.

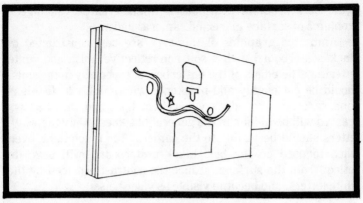

Fig. 6-19. Animated graphic.

Animated Graphics

Figure 6-19 depicts an animated graphic composed of several layers of cardboard. The top layer has windows or slots cut in it to reveal lines or characters painted on the bottom layer as the middle layer is removed. Diagram a lighting arrangement which you feel will correctly illuminate such a graphic.

Lights which are placed above the graphic will cast shadows in the slots and obscure the letters. Lights from below will cast shadows also. Only light from the two sides seems to work if the graphic is made with a noticeable surface reflection. Examine Fig. 6-20 which depicts this setup. In addition, examine Fig. 6-21, in which the results of using such a technique are portrayed.

The shadows are cast at the ends of the slots. This method seems to be the least distracting alternative. Again, a light perpendicular to the graphic would solve the shadow-

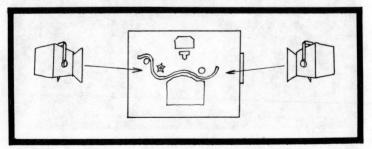

Fig. 6-20. Lighting an animated graphic to eliminate unwanted shadows.

in-the-slots problem best, but it might create even bigger problems of surface glare and camera shadow.

Animated graphics of this type are best constructed of black posterboard with a soft non-reflective finish and white lettering. The edges of the posterboard, especially in the slots, should be cut evenly and blackened with a dull ink. If this is done carefully, no edges will reflect light and the shadows created will be hidden in the general blackness. Only the white letters should be visible to the camera. Too much light, even when focused on the best black posterboard, will begin to reflect from the surface, reduce the contrast provided by the white letters, and become visible as video noise.

GOBOS, TRANSPARENCIES, MODELS

The lighting of flat and multilayered animated graphics is relatively simple when compared with the problems involved in the lighting of gobos, transparencies, and models. The terms "gobo" and "matte" are used to identify two- or three-dimensional frames which are placed between the camera and the scene in order to provide a foreground for the action.

The lighting of gobos, transparencies, and models involves complex depth-of-field problems as well as those associated

Fig. 6-21. Animated graphic illuminated correctly.

134

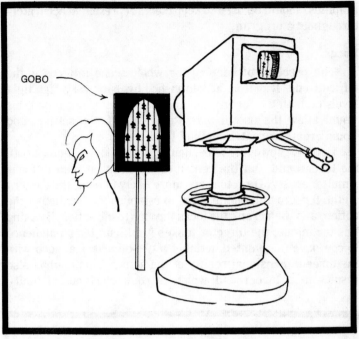

Fig. 6-22. Providing foreground with a gobo.

with the mixing of real and simulated objects in a believable manner. See Fig. 6-22. If the gobo is two-dimensional, that is, if it consists of details painted around an aperature cut in a single piece of posterboard, the lighting problem involves surface reflection, color control, and the appropriate amount of illumination for the effect desired.

Surface Reflection

Consider the problem of surface reflection first. What lighting arrangement would you use to prevent such reflection? Diagram an appropriate setup.

The problem of surface reflection is treated as it was with any flat graphic: Two lights from above and to the sides create an even and shadowless illumination of the surface of the gobo without reflecting light into the lens. Refer to Fig. 6-23.

Color Control

What about the problem of maintaining color control?

The same kinds of lighting instruments, operating at about the same intensities recommended for illuminating flat

135

graphics, should be used to keep colors represented accurately throughout a program.

Focus

The problem of keeping the whole scene in focus is the difficult one. It can be accomplished by using very high light levels on both the foreground and on the center of action. This would allow the use of a relatively high f-stop setting, and would create a greater depth-of-field.

Usually, however, television directors do not require both the foreground and the center of action to be seen in focus simultaneously. Directors are more likely to focus the camera on the foreground, or the gobo, to establish the location of the action, and then crank the focus through to the action. By using this technique, the director makes it difficult for an audience to compare the painted detail of a two-dimensional gobo with the three-dimensional reality of the actors. This method also results in a foreground which is completely out of focus.

Fig. 6-23. Lighting the gobo.

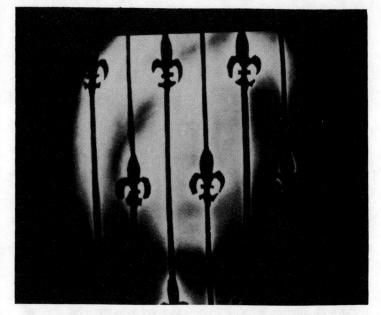
Fig. 6-24. Gobo, in focus, placed in front of subject that is out of focus.

Depending upon the mass of the foreground, however, it may still be visible.

Gobos representing delicate tracery often become virtually invisible when they are in the foreground and out of focus. This is especially true if they are seen in silhouette. Figure 6-24 centers attention on a gobo while the subject remains out of focus in the background. Figure 6-25 reverses the process by showing a subject displayed behind a gobo that is out of focus.

A popular use of a gobo in a theatrical piece involves the combination of a silhouette-type gobo with the projection of a pattern of shadows on the action or the background. It is a simple yet effective technique which requires coordination between the illumination of the background, the acting area, and the gobo in the foreground. See Fig. 6-26.

Notice the separation between the wall in the background, the acting area, and the gobo. The effect depends upon the control of light so that none spills onto the gobo and little falls upon the back wall, except that which is designed to cast the pattern of shadows associated with a barred window.

The major point of this illustration is that each element must be illuminated separately, or not illuminated, as is the

Fig. 6-25. Subject, in focus, displayed behind gobo that is out of focus.

Fig. 6-26. Gobo combined with pattern of shadows cast on background.

Fig. 6-27. Effect of using gobo and pattern of shadows on background.

case with this gobo. As is true with all such scenic effects, success depends upon a coordinated effort: The gobo and the camera must be positioned accurately or the technique will be exposed and the illusion lost. Figure 6-27 captures the live action diagramed in Fig. 6-26.

Overlays

One type of graphic material commonly found in television is the acetate overlay. When using overlays, additional problems of surface reflection are created. Acetate is particularly difficult because the surface is rarely flat enough to eliminate all reflections from it.

Examine Fig. 6-28 which shows the correct method of lighting an overlay or overhead transparency for television. Note that the setup is roughly equivalent to the one used for a gobo.

The use of white or painted scrim introduces a mechanical means of effecting a dissolve between a title card and live action using only one camera. The graphic material is painted on the scrim, or letters are glued into position and it is placed in the standard gobo position. Refer to Fig. 6-29 which serves to visualize the use of such a piece of scrim located in an area

139

Fig. 6-28. Lighting an overlay.

normally reserved for a gobo. If sufficient light is used, the camera can be focused on the scrim rather than on the scene beyond. Refocusing the camera on the acting area, assuming it is also brightly illuminated, then causes the material on the scrim to virtually disappear. This effect can be strengthened by reducing the intensity of the light on the scrim at the same time the camera is being refocused.

Can you think of an appropriate way to light the graphic found in Fig. 6-29?

Fig. 6-29. Painted scrim used instead of gobo.

140

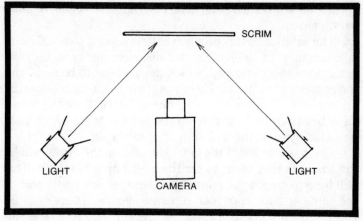

Fig. 6-30. Lighting a scrim.

Figure 6-30 demonstrates the correct method for lighting the scrim. Note the positions of lighting instruments used.

The effective use of such two-dimensional frames as gobos, transparencies, and scrims depends upon the control of the light both in the foreground and in the acting area. Each is illuminated separately because each represents a different set of problems which require different and sometimes mutually exclusive techniques.

Three-Dimensional Models

The use of three-dimensional frames or models as foreground material is generally the most difficult task facing the lighting director with the possible exception of the illumination of models or miniature settings so that live action can be superimposed onto them. Three-dimensional graphics are used when a high degree of realism is desired, or when the viewer is supposed to examine the construction very carefully or ponder its significance. Any lack of craftsmanship in design, construction, or presentation can destroy the effect. The lighting of three-dimensional miniatures which are to be combined with live action will consume more studio time than will any other technique.

One such three-dimensional model is shown in relation to a live action segment in Fig. 6-31. Examine the illustration carefully, and solve the lighting problem implied in the illustration. Jot down the various types of considerations you

141

should be concerned with and diagram the actual lighting arrangement.

The solution to this problem entails several steps. First, it is necessary to determine the distances between the live action, the model through which the action is to be seen, and the camera or cameras. There is no firm rule here because the scale of the model is the determining factor. Once the lenses have been selected, largely on the basis of the fields of view provided by each, the task of lighting can begin.

The basic angle of the *key* light used on the model will be the same as that selected for the acting area beyond it. This will help to create the impression that they are really part of the same scene rather than separate elements. Care must be exercised at this point not to reflect into the lens an inappropriate surface texture on the model. Some compromise within the acting area may be necessary for the sake of unity within the scene as a whole.

Fill light, and even *back* light, should be added to bring out the three-dimensional quality of the model. This is made easier if the model is really a series of planes perpendicular to the camera because that design admits light most readily. Such a model can be seen in Fig. 6-32.

Fig. 6-31. Three-dimensional model viewed from camera and from side.

MODEL

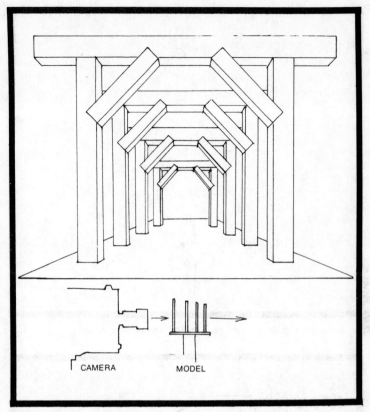

Fig. 6-32. Three-dimensional model comprising a series of planes placed perpendicular to the camera.

Each of the lights used on the model must be diffused if the illusion of reality is to be attained. The camera should be placed extremely close to the model. Contrasts between highlight and shadow will seem harsh and unreal unless they are reduced to a level somewhat less than normal. Figure 6-33 shows the camera location and positioning of the lighting instruments needed.

Sometimes all direct light must be removed from the model, and illumination must be provided only indirectly through reflection from large white cards placed above and to the sides of the model. Obviously, such a construction cannot be moved easily in the studio, and the rest of the program may have to be designed around it. Figure 6-34 diagrams the effect described.

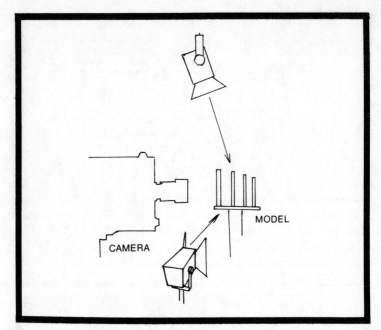

Fig. 6-33. Lighting a three-dimensional model.

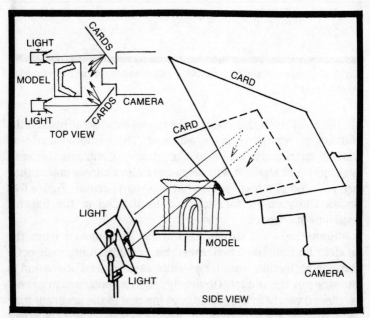

Fig. 6-34. Light reflecting off cards to illuminate a model, viewed from above and from the side.

144

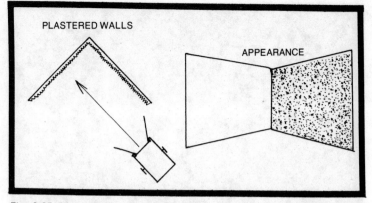

Fig. 6-35. Light eliminating surface texture on one plane, accentuating surface texture on an intersecting plane.

If direct light is used on the model, extreme care must be taken to avoid focusing the camera on these three-dimensional areas on which the actual texture of the model is revealed, because this actual texture will be of a far different scale than that of the live action.

Since there is no way to avoid revealing the actual texture of some part of a three-dimensional model illuminated by direct light, the only solution is to avoid including those portions in the camera's view. The principle is simple: Light, positioned to reduce or eliminate the effect of surface texture on one plane, will actually accentuate the effect of surface texture on an intersecting plane. Placement of lighting instruments to bring about such an effect is shown in Fig. 6-35.

Remember, the surface texture of the model may be a highly reflective varnish used to preserve the model. Such reflections would be quite out-of-step with what was supposed to represent a plaster wall. Unless highly theatrical effects are desired, such as a torch-lit castle in a horror movie, it is often best to diffuse the light falling on the model and to reduce the contrast between highlight and shadow to what seems to be less than normal and less than that created in the acting area framed by the model. Figure 6-36 helps to illustrate this point.

One complicating factor remains: The use of a relatively high level of light intensity on the model in the foreground is necessary if the depth-of-field is to be kept in step with reality. It is difficult to achieve subtle effects when forced to work with high levels of light, but the cameras will require it. The graphic artist can help to a degree by judicious use of an

Fig. 6-36. Diffused light on a model with reduced contrast between highlight and shadow.

airbrush on the model. If some of the light, shadow, and color contrasts are spray painted on the model, the lighting director has an easier task. Again, most television directors will use the models as a special effect and will not dwell on their weaknesses for a long period of time.

SUMMARY

The principles of lighting graphics are the same as those for the human face or scenery. Each type of graphic poses a separate set of problems involving the maintenance of a general level of illumination necessary for the operation of the cameras, the provision of an unchanging quality of light so that colors will be treated uniformly, the selection of positions for the lighting instruments which will facilitate the control of texture-producing highlights and shadows, and the provision of controlled intensities of light in the foreground, acting area, and background so that the appropriate depth-of-field can be achieved.

If you feel that you have mastered the various lighting techniques explained in this chapter, take your newly acquired knowledge to the television studio and practice what you have learned. If you are still unclear on a few points, review the material in this chapter.

Chapter 7
Special
Lighting Effects

Chapter 7
Special
Lighting Effects

Chapter Objectives

   *Given a series of pictures representing the limbo, cameo,
and silhouette effects, the reader will be able to visually identify
each effect and reproduce that effect in an actual television
studio. Given a series of pictures depicting the lighting of
television sets, the reader will be able to visually identify the important variables one should consider when lighting a set, and
describe problems common to each.*

Chapter 7 will acquaint you with several special lighting
effects. Examples of these effects will be presented, followed
by an explanation of how each may be achieved.

   Earlier chapters in this book have explored a number of
basic principles common to television lighting. These
principles have then been applied to standard lighting
arrangements. On occasion, production personnel have found
it necessary to deviate from the norm, thus utilizing qualities
found in special lighting techniques. The development of such
techniques has been fostered by a desire to gain pictorial
emphasis and to stimulate in the viewing audience a positive
emotional response. Audiences have learned to appreciate
their special nature and to expect their use in theatrical
circumstances. These effects are best used as strong visual
accents in a television program.

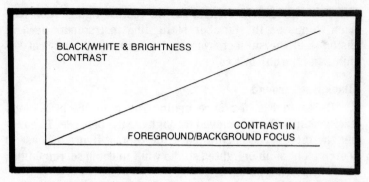

Fig. 7-1. Relationship of focus contrast to black and white contrast.

A discussion involving special lighting effects must consider two dominant aspects of a picture affected by lighting: Contrasts in focus, and contrasts in brightness (black to white on the gray scale).

Foreground, middleground, and background focus contrasts are achieved through manipulation of the depth-of-field of the lens which is, in turn, largely controlled by the amount of light provided. Contrasts in apparent brightness are caused by the range of pigments involved (lights, darks, and hues) and by differing levels of illumination applied to elements within the scene.

Often, black and white contrasts are combined with focus contrasts to provide controlled emphasis within the picture. As is indicated in Fig. 7-1, the more focus contrast provided, the less black and white contrast is likely to be required.

Three special lighting effects commonly found in television production include limbo, cameo, and silhouette. Because these terms vary in title and definition depending upon the locale, we shall present the three effects according to those characteristics common to each.

LIMBO EFFECT

Examine Fig. 7-2. This picture illustrates the effect which we refer to as limbo lighting. Note three aspects of the example: Its black background, the very light nature of the central figure, and the central figure's full three-dimensional presentation.

Take a few minutes to think about how you might control or manipulate each of these three elements. How might you achieve a good black background, a light central figure, and a three-dimensional portrayal of the central figure? Consider such things as the number of lighting instruments needed, distance of the subject from its background, the intensity of light, and the object's color.

Black Background

Refer to Fig. 7-2 once again. The presence of a black background is best achieved through the use of space. To carry out the effect, you should place the central figure at least 10 feet in front of an unlighted studio wall. In doing so, remember three important points:

(1) Do not attempt to use a black surface close to the figure. The surface, regardless of color, will reflect light which will appear in the picture as either a dark gray background, as flecks of light, or as electronic noise. Figure 7-3 illustrates such an effect. Examine it closely. (2) Ambient or spill light creates no problem if the figure illuminated is placed ten or more feet from the background. A problem does arise if the background surface is too close to the central figure. Figure 7-4 shows the effect ambient light has when the subject has been placed too close to the background. Figure 7-5 shows the same ambient light, only in this instance the subject has been placed ten feet from the same background. (3) Remember, light reflected from the central figure to the back wall will

Fig. 7-2. Limbo effect.

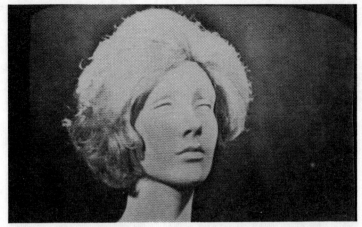
Fig. 7-3. Subject too close to black background.

have to travel past the central figure to the camera, a distance of about 25 feet. The attenuation of light energy is such that the light reaching the camera will be insufficient to be processed by the camera. Figure 7-6 clarifies this problem.

Light Subject

When analyzing factors needed in producing a light central figure, two stand out as the most prominent: The color of the

Fig. 7-4. Effect of ambient light when subject is too close to background.

Fig. 7-5. Effect of ambient light when subject is 10 feet from background.

object, and the intensity of light. In terms of color, a light pigment works best for achieving a limbo effect. It may be necessary to increase the intensity of the light slightly, as compared with the standard three- or four-instrument arrangements, to provide the contrast desired.

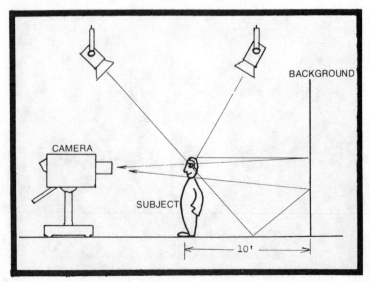

Fig. 7-6. Ambient light traveling far to camera.

Fig. 7-7. Light- and dark-skinned subject viewed under same light conditions.

Remember, however, that arbitrary increases in light intensity often act to reduce the subtleties of shading so essential to a three-dimensional portrayal. Figure 7-7 compares a light-skinned and a dark-skinned subject lit under the same conditions of intensity. Note that the lighter skinned subject fares better under such conditions.

Fig. 7-8. Dark-skinned subject lit under intensity for light-skinned subject.

153

Fig. 7-9. Dark-skinned subject lit under reduced intensity.

Figure 7-8 depicts an interesting problem. How does one light a subject with dark skin under limbo conditions? The solution to such a problem does *not* involve increasing the intensity of the light. It involves selectively *decreasing* it. Examine Figs. 7-8, 7-9, and 7-10. Figure 7-8 shows a dark skinned subject illuminated under the same intensity as Fig. 7-7. Figures 7-9 and 7-10 illustrate the effect of gradually reducing the overall intensity.

Fig. 7-10. Intensity reduced even further.

154

Fig. 7-11. Three-dimensional presentation using three-light arrangement.

If the skin has a highly reflective surface, the problem is even more severe. Subtle shading of the facial contours must be maintained, and a false range of black/white contrasts must be avoided if the limbo effect is to seem believable and consistent with that achieved with other figures of differing pigmentation. In these cases, the effect of special isolation must often be augmented by contrasts in focus.

Three Dimensions

Finally, portraying the central figure in three-dimension is best achieved through the use of a three- or four-instrument arrangement commonly found in static, moving, or multiple camera operation. The figure, especially the human face, should appear realistic and not stylized. Figure 7-11 illustrates the three-dimensional presentation of a central figure using a standard three-light arrangement.

Examine photographs a, b, and c in Fig. 7-12. Which one best illustrates the limbo effect? Choose the photograph that comes closest to meeting our stated description.

Photograph a is the correct answer. Photograph b represents a semi-limbo effect in which the background is presented in medium-dark illumination. Photograph c illustrates a cameo technique, the next special effect we shall discuss.

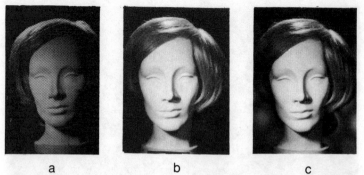

a   b   c

Fig. 7-12. Lighting effects.

CAMEO EFFECT

The second special lighting technique we'll investigate is the "cameo" effect. Refer to c of Fig. 7-12 and note three important characteristics: The presence of a dark, indistinct, or unfocused background: brightly illuminated objects located in the foreground in sharp focus: and a well-illuminated central figure found in the middleground.

If you were called upon to duplicate a cameo effect, what precautions would you take to assure that this technique was achieved? Consider such variables as depth-of-field, focus control, and lighting arrangements.

While attempting to control the three main characteristics found in a cameo effect—the dark or indistinct background, the brightly illuminated foreground objects, and a well-illuminated central middleground figure—a number of factors should be considered.

Dark, Unfocused Background

A dark, unfocused, or indistinct background is best achieved through the control of depth-of-field, since the cameo effect is not dependent upon foreground-to-background color contrasts. Thus, by utilizing telephoto lenses which provide a shallow depth-of-field, a simple adjustment of the camera's focus knob will cause the background to go out of focus and leave foreground objects in sharp focus. Figure 7-13 illustrates the effect of achieving an unfocused background through the shallow depth-of-field characteristics of a telephoto lens. Further clarification of this principle may be seen in Fig. 7-14.

A second procedure for achieving the dark or unfocused background is through reductions of light level and f-stop

Fig. 7-13. Telephoto lens shooting defocused background, focused subject in foreground.

settings of each lens. Such reductions will serve to reduce the depth-of-field of a lens, thus bringing with it a corresponding control of focus. A decrease in light level will, therefore, make it necessary to increase the aperture of a lens (use a larger f-stop number), which carries with it a decrease in the depth-of-field. This decrease in depth-of-field in turn causes

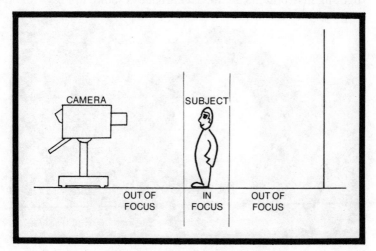

Fig. 7-14. Setup with telephoto lens.

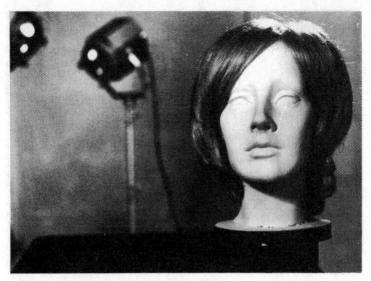

Fig. 7-15. Background defocused through decrease in light intensity.

background and extreme foreground objects to remain out of focus while the middle ground remains in focus. Figure 7-15 illustrates the effect of a reduction in light intensity.

Finally, the placement of separate lighting instruments on the background, taking care to avoid the creation of excessive or multiple shadows, serves to produce the indistinct background effect we are looking for. Focusing of separate lighting instruments on the background is shown in Fig. 7-16.

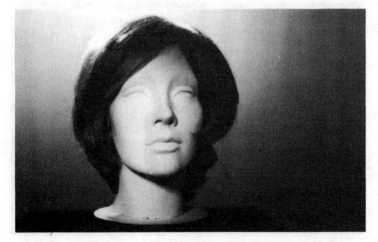

Fig. 7-16. Neutral background illuminated with separate light.

Fig. 7-17. Bright foreground objects through three-light setup.

Bright, Focused Foreground

Producing the effect of brightly illuminated foreground objects in sharp focus is a relatively simple process. One method calls for the use of a standard three- or four-light arrangement on selected foreground figures. The effect of a three-light arrangement is seen in Fig. 7-17. Note the sharpness as well as the brightness of the various objects located in the foreground, while the background remains dark.

Fig. 7-18. Effect of reduced fill light on subject.

A second technique used in enhancing this effect requires the slight lowering of the *fill* light on the subject so as to emphasize the directional quality of the lighting. Figure 7-18 portrays such a mood. Examine the three photographs labeled *a*, *b*, and *c* in Fig. 7-19. One best represents proper cameo lighting. Choose the one which best fits the description. The correct answer is photograph *b*. Photograph *a* shows a limbo effect with the brightly lit subject being placed in front of a black background. Photograph *c* has the cameo characteristics of brightly illuminated foreground objects; however, the background, a textured affair, is also in sharp focus. Only photograph *b* has brightly illuminated foreground objects with a dark indistinct background.

SILHOUETTE EFFECT

The final special lighting effect we will consider is known as silhouette lighting. Examine Fig. 7-20 and note the brightly illuminated background and the darkened foreground. The foreground is recognized only by its outline, details of which act to enrich the picture.

Once again, we would like you to write down your approach to achieving this highly dramatic effect. In your

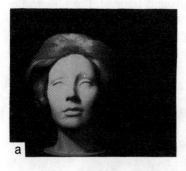

Fig. 7-19. Lighting effects.

Fig. 7-20. Silhouette effect.

answer, consider such things as the ratio of light to dark areas within your picture frame, the placement of lighting instruments to achieve a brightly illuminated background, and the degree of contrast necessary in the foreground areas.

Light/Dark Ratio

The ratio of light areas to dark areas within the frame of each picture, controlled by camera placement and lens

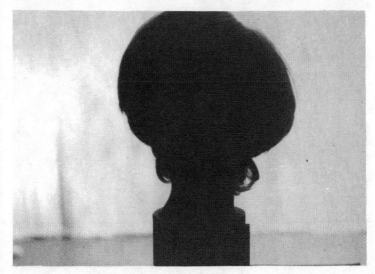

Fig. 7-21. Large area occupied by darkened figure in silhouette.

selection, is of prime importance to this effect. The greater the area of the screen occupied by the darkened figure in the foreground, the greater the amount of electrical energy required for the camera to process the picture; as illustrated in Figure 7-21. The greater the area of the screen occupied by the light background, the less energy required to process the picture, as depicted in Fig. 7-22.

While the lighting of the scene may remain constant, adjustments will have to be made by the technical staff as a camera is used for both closeups (more dark area) and long shots (more light area) of the central subject. The alternative is to adjust the level of illumination on the background as the camera angle is changed. This is generally impractical in studio operations.

Bright Background

The brightly illuminated background should be handled with care, and instruments should not be placed where they will also illuminate actors or objects in the foreground.

The best technique is to separate the foreground area from the background by at least six feet in the case where a rear projection screen is utilized, and about ten feet where realistic set pieces requiring frontal illumination comprise the background. Figure 7-23 shows a set where a rear screen is

Fig. 7-22. Large area occupied by light background, silhouette subject small.

Fig. 7-23. Set utilizing rear screen.

used. Figure 7-24 depicts a set composed of realistic set pieces. The lighting of set pieces will be discussed in a later section of this chapter.

Fig. 7-24. Set utilizing realistic props.

Dark Foreground Figure

Finally, the foreground figure is often kept as dark as possible although a sustained scene, especially one involving the use of closeup camera shots, is best handled with the addition of a trace of *key* light to provide a reflection from a character's eye or to identify prominent features of his face. Figure 7-25 shows the addition of light on a closeup of a subject's face.

Now examine photographs *a, b,* and *c* in Fig. 7-26. Choose the one which best illustrates a silhouette effect.

The answer you should have selected is *a.* Photograph *b* uses a light background of high illumination, however, the foreground subject is partially lighted. Photograph *c,* on the other hand, uses a black background with a partially lighted subject. Only *a* has the necessary characteristics of a highly illuminated background with a subject in complete blackness. Here the concentration is placed on subject outline, with all details of texture, tonal gradation, and modeling being eliminated.

ACCENTUATION OF SET PIECES

Although not considered a special effect, the appropriate illumination of set pieces can go a long way toward enhancing a mood or establishing a scene in which the action is to take place. Because the accentuation of set pieces may be critical

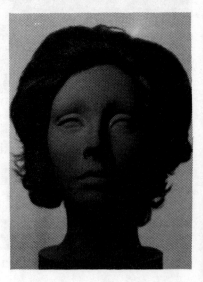

Fig. 7-25. Silhouette with a bit of key light on closeup of subject's face.

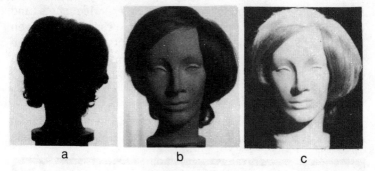

a   b   c

Fig. 7-26. Lighting effects.

to the achievement of an overall lighting effect, it will be considered here. Figure 7-27 illustrates one such example.

Jot down all of the basic considerations you think a lighting director should include when contemplating the lighting of a television set.

Three variables should be considered when lighting set pieces: The layout of the set, which includes such characteristics as size, height, and the presence of objects capable of casting shadows; the shape of set pieces used; and the surface quality of a set.

In those instances where large acting areas contain expansive or large set pieces, problems may arise when the

Fig. 7-27. Accentuation of set pieces through lighting.

script calls for frequent cutting between wide shots and closeups. This will especially be the case when even background illumination is to be maintained. The large number of instruments needed in such instances is often a drawback. Such an effect is shown in Fig. 7-28.

Set Layout

When low angle shots dictate the need for heights of 12 feet or more in set pieces, lighting patterns utilizing back and side

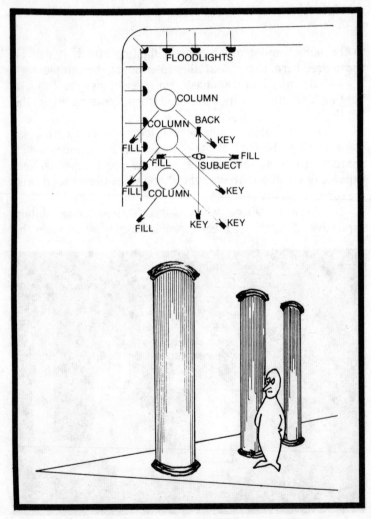

Fig. 7-28. Lighting scheme to enhance columns.

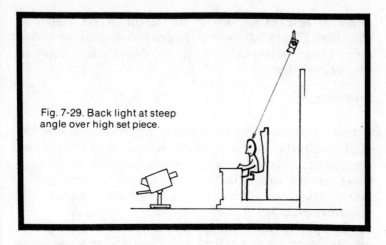

Fig. 7-29. Back light at steep angle over high set piece.

lights often require the placement of these instruments at steep angles. Examine Fig. 7-29, which clarifies this problem.

Finally, when objects that are likely to cast shadows are used, it may be necessary to wash out such shadows. This becomes necessary when the shadows serve to detract from the central action. Figure 7-30 presents such an effect.

Set Shape

The shape of a set may itself cause problems. Sets which are deep or narrow require steep side or back lighting. This

Fig. 7-30. Fills used to wash out shadows cast by set pieces.

condition also exists where the height of set pieces is abnormal. Figure 7-31 depicts the problem. Shallow sets often require head-on lighting, a condition which tends to diminish subject modeling.

Set Finish

Finally, the quality and makeup of a set's finish is of utmost importance when selecting lighting arrangements. High contrasts in tonal qualities and a corresponding diminished modeling effect is caused when extremely dark backgrounds are used. In these cases the subject often appears overly bright and unnatural in appearance. Figure 7-32 illustrates the effect.

In lighting television programs, production personnel must use separate sets of lighting instruments for acting areas and scenery. In addition, they must apply principles to all elements within the scene created with each camera angle.

If you feel that you need additional exposure to the material which deals with special lighting effects, go back and

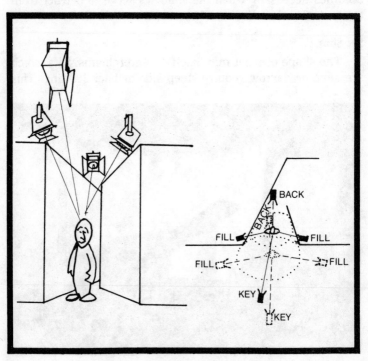

Fig. 7-31. Lighting scheme for narrow set.

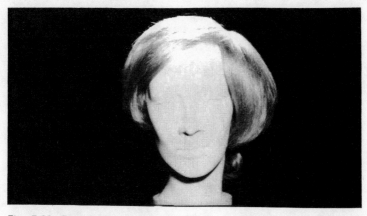

Fig. 7-32. Dark background with high contrast in tonal quality plus diminished modeling.

review the points covered. If you feel that you have mastered the content, try out your knowledge in a live television studio. Practice lighting for the three primary special effects included here: limbo, cameo, and silhouette. Ask your instructor or lighting director to evaluate your work.

Chapter 8

Background Lighting

Chapter Objectives

Given a television studio with lighting instruments, a rear projection screen, and a series of scenic devices a reader will: recognize a number of common problems inherent in lighting a cyclorama and will be able to correct those problems to bring out a desired background and foreground effect; will correctly light a set, keeping all illumination off of the rear screen and thus enhancing its visual effectiveness; will illuminate such devices to create the illusion of realism.

The goal of this chapter is to provide you with information essential to the correct lighting of background areas used in television production.

For our purposes, the term "background" includes scenery, cycloramas, scrims, and rear projection screens. These background areas will be treated separately from the acting area and will require a separate set of lighting instruments. In some studio situations, the floor is also an important scenic element and must receive special treatment.

The background provided for an acting area is designed to clarify aspects of time and place. For example, it might tell the audience that the action is occurring in a railway station, in a television newsroom, or only in its imagination. The background also exists to help the audience see an actor better by creating and maintaining a series of color, texture, and

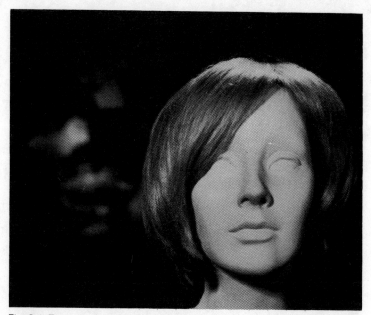

Fig. 8-1. Texture and focus contrasts provided between subject's face and background.

focus contrasts between the actor's face and the background. Figure 8-1 helps to illustrate this point. If the elements in the picture are controlled, prime attention will be on the actor while a secondary emphasis is maintained on his surroundings.

THE CYCLORAMA

The most flexible and popular scenic device which promotes the development of this level of control of the visual elements in television production is the *cyclorama*. An example of a cyclorama is shown in Fig. 8-2.

Physically the cyclorama can be arranged to create a variety of opportunities cleverly disguised as problems for the lighting director. If a series of drapery-type folds are placed in the cyclorama and if it is illuminated from only one side, a series of vertical light-dark stripes will be created. Examine Fig. 8-3 which depicts such an effect.

If the cyclorama is stretched taut and illuminated evenly by a row of floodlights across the top, no discernible shadows will be created at all, and the background will appear as an even and dimensionless expanse. See Fig. 8-4 for this effect.

Fig. 8-2. Cyclorama.

If the cyclorama can be drawn taut so that no folds or wrinkles are present, illuminating it is no problem. Special floodlights have been developed for this purpose. They feature a light-spreading parabolic reflector and no lens. In theory, the

Fig. 8-3. Draped cyclorama lighted from side to produce vertical stripes.

Fig. 8-4. Taut cyclorama, lighted across top to produce shadowless condition.

edge of the light projected from such an instrument will be half the intensity of that in the center of the pattern, thus providing the opportunity to overlap such patterns and create an even illumination of the surface. The lighting instrument described here is shown in Fig. 8-5.

The most perfect shadowless effect would be created by framing the cyclorama with rows of floodlights on the sides as well as on the top and bottom. This technique, used in theatrical make-up mirrors, is generally considered im-

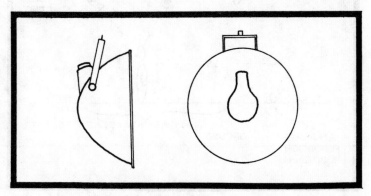

Fig. 8-5. Floodlights used for taut cycloramas.

practical in the television studio. Instead, a row is placed at the top or bottom, or back, depending upon the effect desired. The illumination will be greater on the portion of the cyclorama closest to the instruments. This obvious fact is the key to the creation of the most common effects.

Illumination of the cyclorama from the top will create a background which is light at the top and relatively dark at the bottom. People standing in front of it can be brightly illuminated and, therefore, will appear to stand out from the background. Placing the floodlights at the bottom of the cyclorama will illuminate the lower half more than the upper and create opportunities to view performers in silhouette. This latter technique is particularly effective in dance presentations.

These effects depend upon the separation of the background from the acting area, so that light from the acting area does not wash out the effect on the cyclorama or project distracting shadows upon it.

Figure 8-6 illustrates two positions for floodlights designed to illuminate the cyclorama from below. Placement of the instruments on the floor in front of the cyclorama generally requires the use of camera angles which do not reveal the floor or an actor's full figure, or the use of a *ground row*, which is a low wall placed in front of the lights to keep them from view. Placement of the floodlights behind the cyclorama solves the

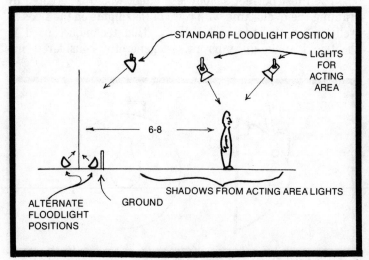

Fig. 8-6. Positions for floodlights designed to light cyclorama from below.

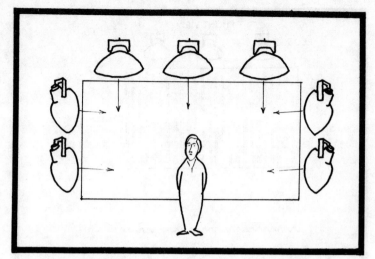

Fig. 8-7. Lighting of damaged cyclorama.

ground row problem but acts both to reduce the apparent brightness of the background and to reveal any seams or irregularities in the canvas out of which the cyclorama is constructed.

All too often, the cyclorama is not in perfect condition, and several floodlights will have to be placed in such a way that they intentionally wash out the shadows cast from wrinkles, seams, or by the instruments illuminating it. This need not act to increase the light reflected from the cyclorama because the same number of instruments can be used. The real problem created by a damaged cyclorama is one of hiding the instruments on the sides or on the floor behind the actor, or restricting camera angles to those which do not include the corrective floodlights. Figure 8-7 illustrates such a lighting arrangement.

Unfortunately, such corrections often require a trial-and-error use of valuable studio time and the reblocking of the cameras. It might prove better to develop a different background effect than to persist in the attempt to make an inferior cyclorama look better than it is.

The appearance of softly folded draperies to form a background is created by folding a cyclorama, located in a large studio, and placing a row of floodlights approximately ten feet from its top edge. This would place the instruments over the acting area, but no problems would be caused if the

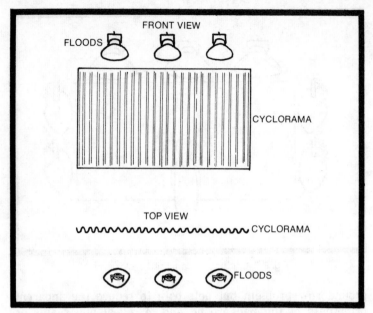

Fig. 8-8. Light placement for softly folded draperies.

light was all directed at the cyclorama and not down at the acting area itself. Examine Figs. 8-8 and 8-9, both of which illustrate the effect described.

Fig. 8-9. Softly folded draperies created by placing floodlights along top of cyclorama.

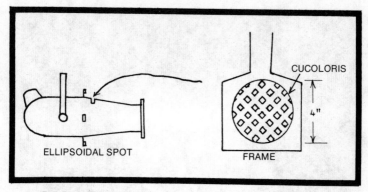

Fig. 8-10. Ellipsoidal spotlight with slot for cucoloris in frame.

No extreme angles are necessary in the creation of this drapery effect if the folds in the cyclorama are relatively full. The richest drapery effect is created by using three times as much material as that required if the cyclorama were stretched taut. The more shallow the folds, the greater the angle to the side required in the positioning of the instruments.

The "Cookie"

Patterns of light and shadow can be projected upon the cyclorama by several types of spotlights and pattern devices. A variety of geometric patterns can be created through the use of an ellipsoidal spotlight and a *cucoloris*, or "cookie," so called because it is a circular piece of metal about four inches in diameter out of which the desired pattern has been cut. The cookie is placed in a frame and inserted into the spotlight through opening provided for that purpose. The ellipsoidal spot and cucoloris are shown in Fig. 8-10.

This pattern of light and shadow is most visible when it is projected upon a darkened cyclorama. Generally, such projections are combined with a low level of illumination on the cyclorama so that the background effect has less light-dark contrast within it than does the image of the actor performing in front of it. Figure 8-11 illustrates this effect.

The Flag

The ellipsoidal spot is favored for this purpose because it casts a narrow and more intense beam than does the adjustable Fresnel spotlight. Because the pattern device is internally mounted, it is a simpler instrument to handle. The

179

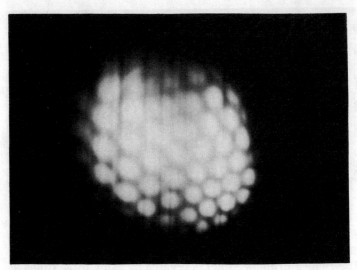

Fig. 8-11. Pattern design produced by ellipsoidal spot focused on darkened cyclorama.

Fresnel is not engineered to permit the use of a cucoloris and therefore will not project or focus a pattern if placed between the internal lamp and the lens. Consequently, any such projections using the Fresnel require the use of an externally positioned pattern device, sometimes called a "flag" or gobo. This external pattern device is shown in Fig. 8-12. The flag or

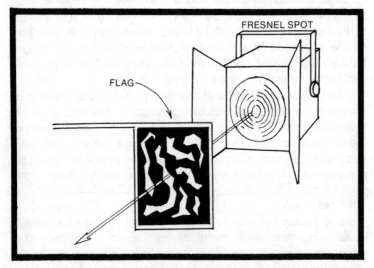

Fig. 8-12. Flag positioned in front of Fresnel spotlight.

180

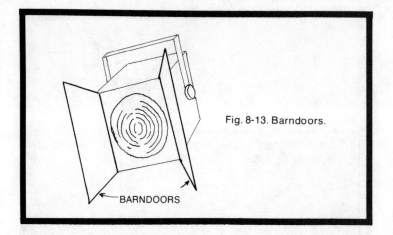

Fig. 8-13. Barndoors.

BARNDOORS

gobo must be positioned some distance from the Fresnel spotlight so that the edge of the shadows cast will be in focus. The farther from the instrument the flag is placed, the sharper the focus will be. Of course, positioning the flag far from the Fresnel reduces the size of the projected shadow pattern, and a larger gobo may be required. The projection of a pattern across a large expanse of cyclorama would require a combination of very intense light sources and flags placed relatively close to those light sources. "Barndoors," or metal flaps hinged to the front of the lighting instrument, would probably be required to keep the light off the acting areas. These barndoors can be seen in Fig. 8-13.

The shadow pattern projected by a Fresnel will be difficult to focus. Also, given the usual position of the light source above and approximately 20 feet away from the cyclorama, the top and bottom of the pattern will often be out of focus while the center remains in focus. This is due to the different distances the shadow is projected. Examine Fig. 8-14 which serves to clarify this point. In this case, the image projected is subject to distortion: The greater the distance from the light source, the larger the image. This factor could be reduced if the light source were placed at a point perpendicular to the center of the cyclorama. However, this technique is not used because actors, cameras, microphones, and studio personnel would all cast shadows on the cyclorama. Consequently, the distortions caused by positioning the light source on the grid is accepted and the television director invents ways to shoot around the most severely distorted areas.

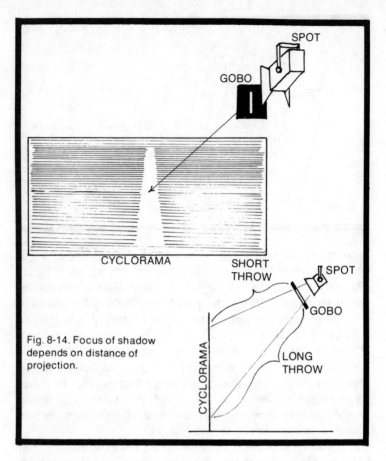

Fig. 8-14. Focus of shadow depends on distance of projection.

Review

At this point in our exercise we will review the material covered. You will be presented with a series of illustrations depicting a particular lighting setup. For each lighting setup found in the script, you will be presented with a photograph which shows the end result of that arrangement. Your job will be to match each illustration with its corresponding photograph.

Check your answers with the correct ones provided:

1. Fig. 8-15—Fig. 8-22
2. Fig. 8-16—Fig. 8-20
3. Fig. 8-17—Fig. 8-21
4. Fig. 8-18—Fig. 8-24
5. Fig. 8-19—Fig. 8-23

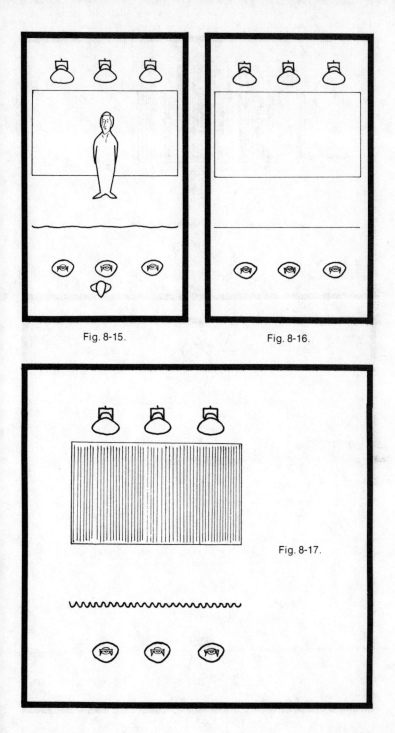

Fig. 8-15.

Fig. 8-16.

Fig. 8-17.

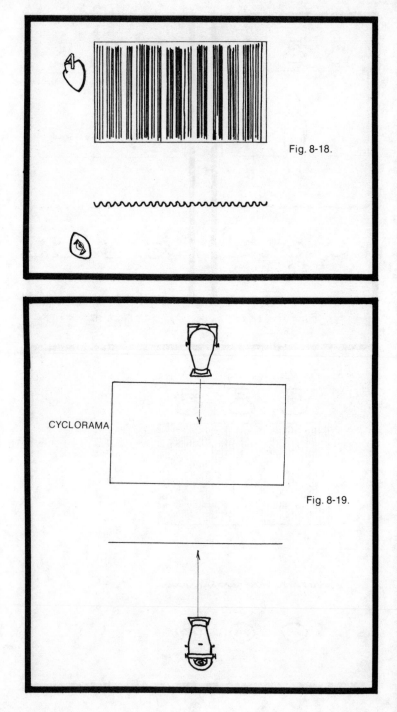

Fig. 8-18.

CYCLORAMA

Fig. 8-19.

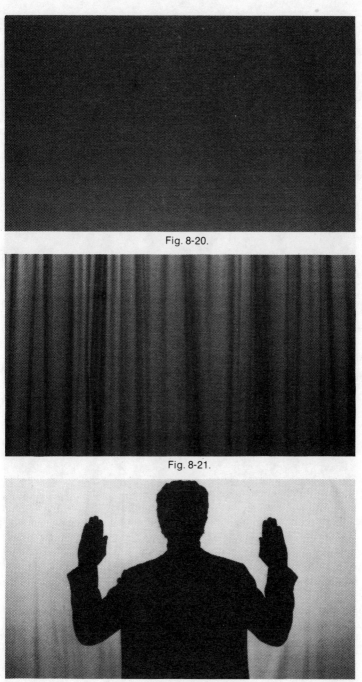

Fig. 8-20.

Fig. 8-21.

Fig. 8-22.

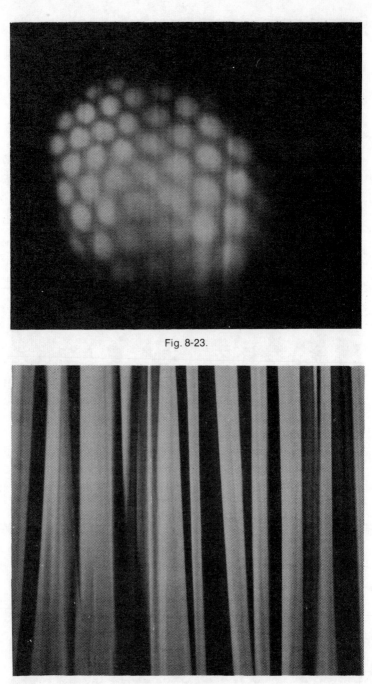

Fig. 8-23.

Fig. 8-24.

THE REAR PROJECTION SCREEN

While the light source used to project shadow patterns on the background is not placed perpendicular to the cyclorama, solid, or opaque walls, it can be placed in that position behind a rear projection screen. The rear projection screen is made out of a relatively transluscent plastic and is designed to facilitate the projection of photographs, generally in 2×2 or 35mm format, on the rear wall of the acting area without casting shadows of the actor on the same wall or destroying the effect of the lights focused on him. Figure 8-25 illustrates the arrangement of subject and lighting when utilizing a rear projection screen.

Figure 8-26 shows an actor in relation to a rear projection screen, which serves to supply the necessary background needed in a particular situation.

Positioning

Once the projector or spotlight is positioned so that the image or shadow pattern covers the desired area of the rear

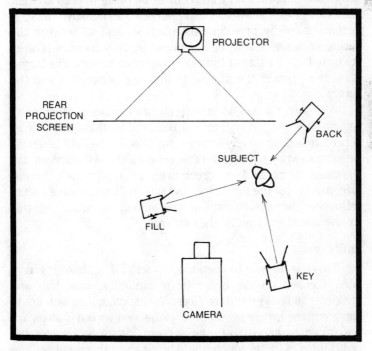

Fig. 8-25. Arrangement of subject and lighting when utilizing a rear projection screen.

Fig. 8-26. Actor with rear projection screen for background.

projection screen, every effort must be made to keep all light off the front side of that screen. Primarily, this is accomplished by providing as much separation between the acting area and the screen as possible. This distance is often governed by the size of the rear projection screen. The larger it is, the greater the allowable distance between it and the actors.

A problem arises as the screen size increases. Many more footcandles of light energy are required to illuminate a large screen to a desired level than a small one. The light level can be increased by placing the projector closer to the screen, but the closer it is, the less screen area it can illuminate. Screen size, position of the projector, and screen illumination all act to influence the positioning of the acting area, its lighting instruments, and finally, the cameras.

Spill Light

There is no way to keep the *key* and *fill* lights which have been focused on the actor from continuing past him and striking the background or floor. This spilling light will act to wash out the image on the rear projection screen if steps are not taken to keep it off the screen. Figure 8-27 shows the positioning of lights which would bring about this problem. The problem itself is depicted in Fig. 8-28.

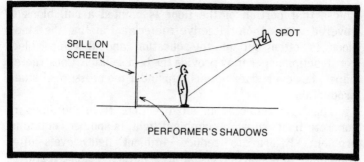

Fig. 8-27. Spill light projected on rear projection screen.

The first step in preventing the problem is to place the actor no closer than six feet from the screen so that the spill washes out only the lower (and presumably less important) portion of the picture.

Second, the barndoors on the *fill* and *key* lights should be used to reduce the area illuminated. Ideally, the actor should be placed about ten feet in front of the screen so that no light spills onto it. Remember, this requires the use of a larger screen and a stronger projector. Correct placement of lights and actor in relation to the rear screen is shown in Fig. 8-29.

The acting area lights will illuminate the studio floor at the base of the rear screen and will likely wash out the picture

Fig. 8-28. Washed out rear screen image behind actor because of spill light.

unless that portion of the floor is painted a dull black or covered with a non-reflective material. Painting the studio floor is often out of the question and therefore black construction paper may provide the best solution. Construction paper, however, does not hold up under the pressure of studio production.

The light reflected in all directions from the standard concrete floor, known as ambient light, is another continuing problem. Efforts to reduce ambient light levels often contribute to a sharper visual presentation and one featuring good light-dark contrast and a full range of intermediate grays or brightnesses. Too much ambient light washes out the dark tones and results in a flat, less dynamic picture.

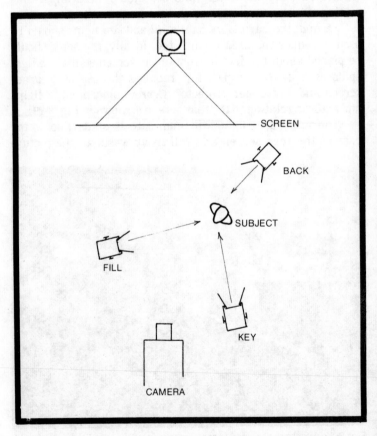

Fig. 8-29. Correct placement of lights and subject in relation to rear screen.

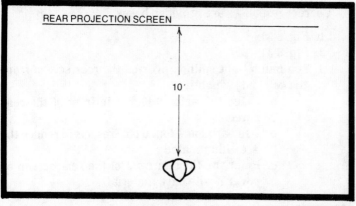

Fig. 8-30.

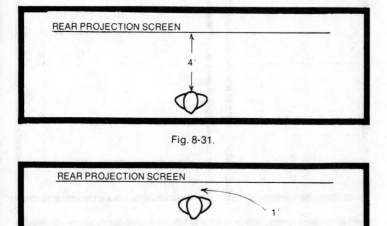

Fig. 8-31.

Fig. 8-32.

Review

To evaluate your expertise, take a few minutes to answer the following questions.

1. Which of the illustrations in Figs. 8-30, 8-31, and 8-32, used to identify physical arrangements for setting up a rear projection screen is correct?
2. Which of the rear screens in Figs. 8-33, 8-34, and 8-35 would require the greatest number of footcandles for proper illumination?
3. Identify the source of the problem illustrated in Fig. 8-36 and suggest ways of correcting it.

Correct responses are provided below:

1. Fig. 8-30
2. Fig. 8-35
3. Too much light spilling over on the rear screen from the *key* and *fill* lights.
   a. Place the actor 6-10 feet in front of the rear screen.
   b. Use barndoors found on Fresnels to reduce the area illuminated.
   c. Paint the floor in front of the rear screen or cover it with dark material.

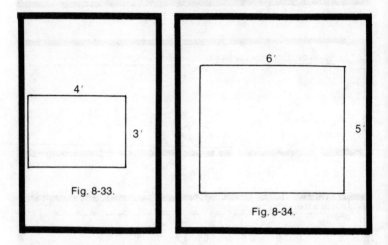

Fig. 8-33.

Fig. 8-34.

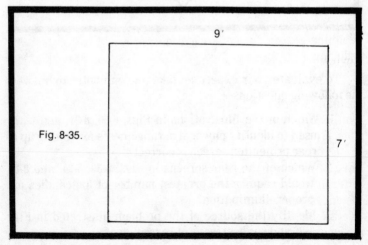

Fig. 8-35.

Fig. 8-36.

ATMOSPHERE ENHANCERS

This chapter's final area of concern centers around techniques for illuminating those scenic devices required for adding realism or enhancing a certain mood or feeling within a given setting.

While the electronic effects characteristic of television reduce or eliminate the need for scrim or gauze in the studio as a means of accomplishing dissolves, some scenic effects are still best produced through the control of light. Backgrounds depicting exterior scenes, such as sunsets, involve not only reducing the intensity of the illumination but lowering the angle of the lighting instruments as well. Examine Figs. 8-37 and 8-38. The first shows our subject illuminated from a normal 45° angle. The second photograph shows the subject illuminated from a 90° angle, which would be appropriate at sunrise and sunset.

Exteriors, such as forests or crowded streets, are best created by lighting and painting areas far from the camera differently from those closest to the camera. In such scenes, distances are commonly distinguished on the basis of color fidelity, focus, diminishing size, and movement. The clever designer manipulates these elements to suggest distance

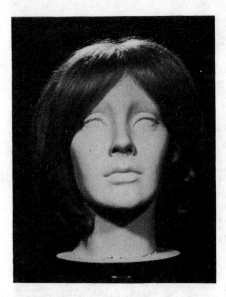

Fig. 8-37. Model illuminated from 45° angle.

where there is little. Generally, objects in the distance seem illuminated less than those close by.

Added realism can be achieved by dividing the background into zones or planes on the basis of distance from the camera. Also, by allowing one or more intermediate zones to seem darker and, therefore, act as a frame for the most

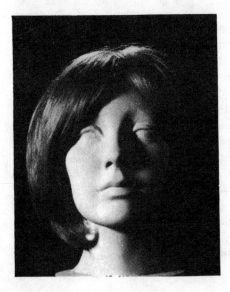

Fig. 8-38. Model illuminated from 90° angle.

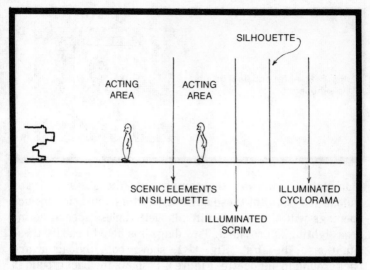

Fig. 8-39. Use of zones to identify distances from camera.

distant zones, which might be illuminated more brightly. Figures 8-39 and 8-40 illustrate such a use of zones to identify varying distances from the camera.

A similar technique can be applied to the lighting of interiors. Backing behind door and window openings can be

Fig. 8-40. Realistic action using multiple planes.

195

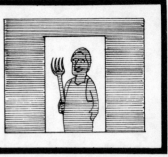

Fig. 8-41. Actor and background in silhouette.

illuminated in a way that emphasizes the shape and any silhouetted detail of those openings. Actors appearing in such openings will also be seen in silhouette unless special acting area lighting is provided. Two diagrams help to clarify these situations. The first, Fig. 8-41, shows both the actor and background in silhouette. Figure 8-42 shows the background in silhouette while the actor is illuminated.

The principle of light-dark contrast can be applied to any acting area as is shown in Figs. 8-43 and 8-44. Actors can be seen in total silhouette, which means they are not illuminated at all, or some light can be provided to reveal the actors' form while maintaining the overall effect of the silhouette.

The angle of background lighting is also important. Only one set of shadows should be evident in exterior scenes. This is accomplished by illuminating the three-dimensional elements in the background with *key*, *fill*, and *back* light as is done in the acting areas. All *key* lights should be placed so the highlights and shadows throughout the scene seem created by the same light source.

While only one set of shadows is desired in interior scenes, the source of light causing a particular shadow is often meant

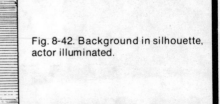

Fig. 8-42. Background in silhouette, actor illuminated.

Fig. 8-43. Actors in total silhouette.

to be in the room itself. If the interior has a single light source, all shadows should be arranged to seem to be cast by that single light source. See Fig. 8-45.

If the interior is to appear to be illuminated by several sources, each should key the shadows in its vicinity. Multiple

Fig. 8-44. Some actors in silhouette, some illuminated.

Fig. 8-45. Shadows on interior scene emanating from single source.

light sources with their separate shadow patterns are depicted in Fig. 8-46.

The confusion generated by unwanted multiple shadows is apparent in Fig. 8-47. This is not an important factor unless a

Fig. 8-46. Shadows on interior scene emanating from multiple light sources.

Fig. 8-47. Effect of multiple shadows.

wide shot of the entire scene is to be used. In a series of closeups, the audience will not notice an inconsistent shadow pattern as long as there is a consistency between the *key* light on the actor and the *key* light on three-dimensional objects within the picture.

The same principle of lighting applies to both actors and three-dimensional objects, including realistic scenery. While

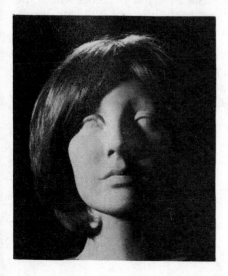

Fig. 8-48.

they must be illuminated separately for optimum control and the elimination of distracting shadows, the lighting must be coordinated so that a unity of effect is achieved.

REVIEW

Take a few minutes to complete the questions which follow.

1. What four key elements are readily used by television set designers to enhance the illusion of distance?
2. Lighting technicians desiring to simulate sunsets as shown in Fig. 8-48 must perform two tasks. What are they?
3. In lighting exterior scenes, it is generally recommended that only one set of shadows be present. How would you accomplish such a feat?

The correct answers follow:

1. Color fidelity, focus control, diminishing size, and movement are the key elements used in distinguishing distances in television settings.
2. To simulate sunsets in exterior scenes, one should reduce the overall illumination in addition to lowering the angle of the lighting instruments used.
3. To maintain one set of shadows while lighting an exterior scene, the lighting director should attempt to illuminate all three-dimensional elements within the background by using *back*, *key*, and *fill* lights, which are separate from those used for the actors.

If you feel that you have mastered the objectives listed in the initial portion of this chapter, your job is over. If further review is needed, retrace those sections where you feel additional practice is needed.

Chapter 9
Remote Telecasts

Chapter Objectives

Given a portable television unit including a camera, video tape recorder. and lighting instruments. the reader will correctly illuminate a scene located outside the television studio. identify common problems associated with lighting for remote telecasts. and will provide corrective solutions to those problems.

All previous discussions in this book have centered around television productions originating from a studio. There are times, however, when a decision arises to forego the controlled conditions associated with the studio and to venture into the uncertainties of producing a television program on location.

As broadcast news organizations have demonstrated, an interview with a scientist is often more effective in the laboratory than it is in a live studio. Similarly, others possessing special knowledge or position may warrant the out-of-studio expenditures of time and energy on the part of television production personnel.

Producing quality programs outside the studio is expensive. This expense is intensified when one considers the special production equipment and techniques required to conduct on-site programs.

Fig. 9-1. Vidicon lag.

The attempt to move 1,000 pound studio camera units to a remote location on a regular basis is impractical because of the time and energy involved. In the world of black-and-white and color television, several portable camera systems have been developed for such out-of-studio use. Most of this equipment is designed around the non-broadcast quality vidicon tube.

Vidicon cameras require twice the intensity of light needed to operate the image-orthicon tube found in most black-and-white studio cameras. If this extra light is not provided, the vidicon camera will produce a poor picture marked by excessive noise or graininess. Conversely, if too much light is focused on white or metallic objects which reflect light sharply, vidicon "lag" will result. This lag is a condition of image retention which forms a distracting comet-effect around the movement of each bright object or reflection. Figure 9-1 shows the effect.

Vidicon cameras, videotape recorders, and lighting instruments associated with productions on location are designed to operate on 110-volt electrical power which is readily available in buildings. Battery-operated models of the Port-a-Pac variety make production possible in places where no electrical power is available. One such portable unit is illustrated in Fig. 9-2.

The most popular lighting instruments for remote productions are those with quartz lamps. These generally lack lenses, possess a variable beam from flood to spot, and come equipped with floorstands. Such instruments are lightweight and portable. In addition, they produce an intense white light which tends to generate considerable heat.

BRIGHTNESS PROBLEMS

The amount of light emitted from these instruments represents both a strength and weakness. In terms of their light weight, portability, ability to function with standard electrical power, and high output, they are considered a real bargain.

Their brightness, however, often creates problems. When the instruments are moved away from the action so as to decrease the high intensity, cameras or additional production equipment may be placed in front of the lamps. This casts shadows upon the actor or objects being illuminated. Figure 9-3 illustrates this problem.

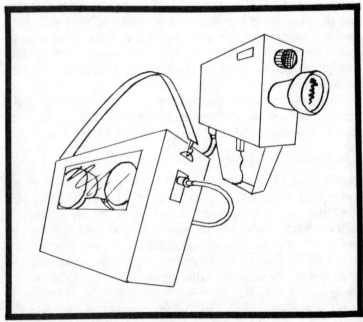

Fig. 9-2. Portable camera equipment.

Fig. 9-3. Shadows cast by TV equipment placed in front of lights.

Also, since the portable lighting instruments are floor mounted, it is difficult to maintain an appropriate angle as they are placed further from the primary scene. The resultant effect, as the instruments are placed on an angle close to eye level, is generally a loss of modeling.

Finally, shadows from the actors are often cast on the back wall rather than on the floor. Figure 9-4 illustrates the eye level angle of the instruments. The resultant shadow of the actor is cast on the background and there is a subsequent loss of modeling.

Fig. 9-4. Lighting instruments placed at eye level casting shadows on the background.

CONTRAST PROBLEMS

The intensity of remote lighting instruments sometimes creates a gray scale problem. The contrast between the bright highlights and shadows is such that most portable television equipment cannot maintain the intermediate grays. Thus, a method is needed to reduce the contrast level to avoid distracting shadows and the flat, dimensionless effect of frontal lighting.

One technique has been devised which is worth considering in most situations. Can you think what it might be?

The trick is not to focus the light on the actors or scene but to direct it to off-camera walls and ceilings which will reflect and diffuse it, thereby adding to the available ambient light. While some modeling is lost, the gray scale remains believable, and distracting shadow patterns are avoided. This technique works with highly reflective white walls and ceilings. It is less effective with dark surfaces. The technique is illustrated in Fig. 9-5.

In some instances where this arrangement is utilized, it may be necessary to place white reflectors off camera to add to the general illumination. Full size sheets of white posterboard may be used.

PLACEMENT PROBLEMS

Placing television actors or interviewees in front of a wall is common practice; it also tends to create lighting problems. Can you think of any such problems? Jot down your answers on a piece of paper.

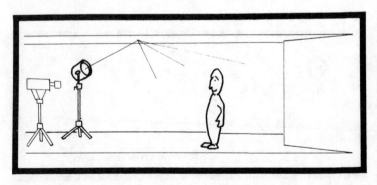

Fig. 9-5. Lighting instruments directed to off-camera ceiling, reflecting onto subject.

Fig. 9-6. Actor in silhouette against bright background.

In addition to the shadow problem, the producer faces a problem of controlling the relative brightness of the wall as compared to that of the actor. If the wall is lighter and brighter than the actor, the actor will appear to be somewhat silhouetted and the facial details will become lost in a general darkening of his face. Figure 9-6 illustrates this effect.

Devise a method for counteracting the previous problem. Again, jot your answer down on a piece of paper.

Placing the actor far from the offending wall or better yet, in a hallway, solves this problem. Since this technique might seem to place the actor in limbo and therefore defeat the purpose for choosing the location in the first place, it will help to place the actor at an outside corner in the hallway or at least next to the important wall rather than in front of it as is shown in Fig. 9-7. The visual effect of such placement is shown in Fig. 9-8. The various lighting techniques identified in previous chapters should be applied wherever possible in remote telecasts. For example, good visual variety can be achieved by placing the skin and fabric textures of the actor's clothes in contrast to the brick, stone, or wood paneling of a specific building. Blocking the action so that it occurs on the z-axis, to and from the camera, rather than from side to side, will increase the dynamic quality of the production and provide the

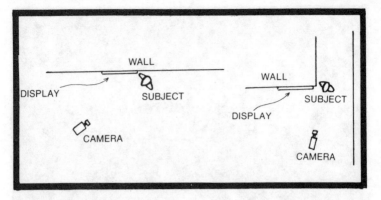

Fig. 9-7. Subject in sketch at left is vulnerable to shadow or silhouette problems. One at right is made safer from these problems by placement in front of hallway.

audience with a realistic or first-person quality rare in most studio productions. This point is further clarified in Fig. 9-9.

ADDITIONAL PROBLEMS

Producing programs on location requires the television producer-director to allow for problems already identified in previous chapters of this text. In addition, several other problems may arise. Can you think of any additional ones?

Fig. 9-8. Actor illuminated in outside hallway, from corner position.

START

ADJUST FIELD OF VIEW
AS SUBJECT APPROACHES

Fig. 9-9. Action is blocked to occur on z-axis, to and from camera.

Additional problems found in remote productions center around the position of the sun, atmospheric conditions, the presence of water or other highly reflective surfaces, and the lack of electricity. If an actor is placed in direct sunlight, severe highlight-shadow problems will be created on his or her face. As a result, intermediate grays will be lost and with them, most of the facial detail.

If an actor is placed in the shadow of overhanging foliage, care must be taken not to silhouette him against a bright sky or sunlit building. Again, facial detail will be diminished. See Fig. 9-10 for a visual representation of this effect.

The best conditions for television productions occurring outdoors generally exist on an overcast day which has general brightness but no direct sunlight. This condition can be approximated on a sunny day through the use of large white cards which reflect and diffuse the sunlight. These reflectors can be arranged to act as a system of *fill* lights which reduce

Fig. 9-10. Actor in silhouette against bright background building.

the shadow contrast and increase the general illumination in a given scene.

Such sunlight reflectors are also valuable in that they can maintain a consistency of color temperature throughout a scene. This is an important factor in color television. (See Chapter 5).

Sketch an illustration which could be used for arranging white card reflectors in such a manner that sunlight would be diffused, thus reducing the shadow contrast of a given scene. Once you have completed the illustration, check your answer with that found in Fig. 9-11.

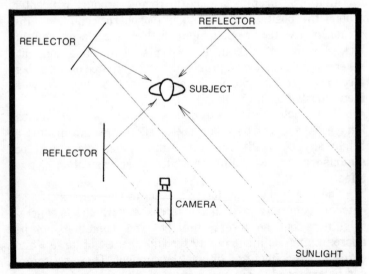

Fig. 9-11. Placement of white card reflectors to diffuse sunlight.

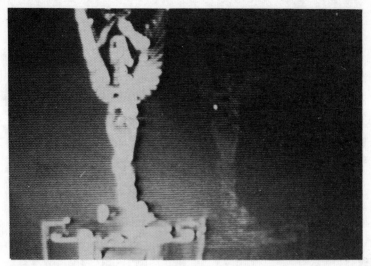

Fig. 9-12.

REVIEW QUESTIONS

A brief review will now be provided for self-evaluative purposes. Answer each of the questions which follow and check your responses with those provided.

1. Identify the problem depicted in Fig. 9-12 and provide a solution for correcting the situation.
2. Identify the problem shown in Fig. 9-13 and provide a method for alleviating the effect.
3. Diagram a technique for reducing the contrast level caused by overly intense remote lighting instruments, which will avoid distracting shadows and the flat illumination found in head-on lighting.
4. Identify the problem found in Fig. 9-14 and diagram a method for counteracting the effect.
5. In producing television programs outdoors, ideal conditions exist on a day which is marked by overcast skies. T F
6. List the various uses of large white cards in connection with remote television productions.

Compare your responses with the correct ones which follow.

1. Figure 9-12 demonstrates the problem of camera "lag" caused by focusing too much light on bright

metallic objects. The problem can be solved by applying a dulling spray and reducing the intensity of the lighting instruments used. In addition, changing the angle of the lighting instruments is likely to help.

2. Figure 9-13 illustrates the problem of picture noise or graininess caused by too little illumination on the remote set. Increasing the degree of illumination should counteract this problem.

3. Figure 9-5 represents the correct answer.

4. Figure 9-14 illustrates the effect of silhouetting an actor against a bright background. Figure 9-7 represents one method of correcting the situation.

5. T

6. Large white cards in remote productions have the following uses:

   a. They serve as *fill* lights to reduce shadow contrast and to increase the general illumination of a given scene.

   b. They help to maintain a consistency of color temperature important in those instances where color portable equipment is employed.

   c. They reflect and diffuse sunlight, thus reducing intensity on overly bright sunny days.

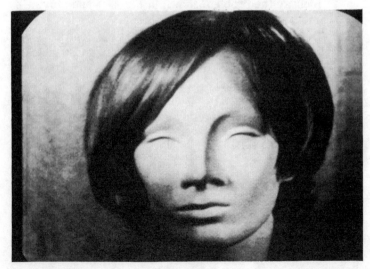

Fig. 9-13.

Fig. 9-14.

SUMMARY

In remote productions, the principles of television lighting remain the same. Only the situation changes. The producer choosing to record materials outside the studio must maintain the visibility of both the location and the actors. This is sometimes difficult when the light is uncontrolled.

Lighting instruments have been developed to provide sufficient illumination for portable camera units, but they are as capable of creating serious visual problems as they are of solving them. Reflectors are often most useful for diffusing light and filling shadows both for interior and exterior work.

Finally, care must be taken to control the overall brightness of a scene, or at least to keep the actor's face the brightest element in the scene unless the theatrical effect of a silhouette is desired.

If you feel that you have mastered the objectives specified in this chapter, practice the various techniques described here and, if possible, have a qualified lighting expert evaluate your work. Should you feel that further reading is necessary, repeat the appropriate sections found in this chapter.

Glossary

additive color system—A system used to explain the mixture of colored light. White light is created when all frequencies in the visible spectrum are added together.

ambient light—An extraneous or unwanted light which often tends to wash out or overly illuminate portions of a television set. Such light is generally caused by a failure to control a light source or reflective surfaces and to keep it confined to those areas for which it was intended.

aspect ratio—A term used for identifying the vertical and horizontal dimensions of a television screen which is three units high by four units wide.

back light—A source of light which is placed directly behind a subject and whose primary function is to separate the subject from the background by rimming the hair and shoulders.

barndoor—A hinged four-piece metal fitting, attached to the front of a Fresnel spotlight, the purpose of which is to control the direction or beam of light projected from the instrument.

base illumination—An overall non-directional level of illumination, measured in footcandles, which is required to activate a pickup tube found in a television camera. The studio base illumination requirements will increase or decrease depending upon the type of pickup tube employed.

cameo—A special lighting technique characterized by a dark or indistinct unfocused background, a well--illuminated middleground central figure, and one or more brightly illuminated foreground objects.

chiaroscuro—A common lighting technique used to convey a feeling of solidarity and to bring out the three dimensional qualities of an object. To achieve such an effect, highlights and shadows are placed along the natural lines or contours of the object being illuminated.

color temperature—A term used to describe the degree of whiteness of a light source measured in degrees Kelvin (°K). Color temperature generally ranges on a continuum from low to high as the color of light goes from a reddish-yellow to a bluish cast. In color television, 3200°K represents a standard industry rating for classifying a light source's degree of whiteness.

contrast range—A term for classifying relative degrees of brightness within a given set (light to dark) in which a television camera is capable of reproducing simultaneously. Pickup tubes used in color television cameras vary in contrast range from a low of 10:1 to a high of 30:1.

cucolorus—A circular piece of perforated metal approximately four inches in diameter which is placed in a special frame and inserted in an ellipsoidal spotlight. A shadow pattern corresponding to the perforations is projected on the scenic background by the instrument.

cyclorama—A large curtain generally extending around the outer limits of a television studio. Such a curtain is used to achieve varying background effects.

depth-of-field—That area, viewed by a lens, which possesses the characteristic of sharp focus; *depth-of-field* increases with the selection of short focal length (wide angle) lenses, by decreasing the aperature of a given lens, and by increasing the distance from camera to subject.

diffuser—A device generally consisting of scrim encased in a wire mesh, which is designed to fit on the front of a scoop, thus reducing the intensity of light emitted from that instrument.

dimmer—An electronic board or panel designed to control the brightness or intensity of a television lighting instrument by reducing the electrical power to that instrument.

ellipsoidal spot—A high intensity spotlight possessing a narrow beam of light which is equipped with an internally mounted pattern device for purposes of projecting designs or patterns on a background.

fill light—A supplementary light placed opposite the *key*, whose primary function is to reduce the shadow cast by the correct placement of the *key*.

flag—An external pattern device designed to work in conjunction with a Fresnel spotlight.

focal length—The distance measured in millimeters or inches from a lens's optical center to the face of a camera pickup tube located directly behind it.

footcandle—A unit of measurement for quantifying the degree of illumination produced by a lamp or reflected from a surface.

Fresnel spot—A standard television lighting instrument characterized by its relative small size, high intensity output, and spot focusing device allowing its beam to be flooded or pinned to a sharply defined area.

f-stop—A series of calibrations or numbers found on a camera lens which control the size of the aperture or opening of that given lens. Small *f-stop* numbers indicate large aperture openings while large *f-stop* numbers indicate smaller openings.

gobo—A two- or three-dimensional frame which is placed between the camera and scene to be photographed for purposes of providing a foreground reference for the action.

gray scale—A scale used in television for designating reflectance values for TV black to TV white with various intermediate steps of *gray* in between. The standard scale used has ten steps.

grid—A series of tracks, pipes, or cross pieces located in or near the studio ceiling designed for suspending television lighting instruments.

ground row—Low scenery approximately two feet in height which is placed on the floor parallel to the bottom of a cyclorama. The functions of such scenery are to complete the scenic effect and to hide floodlights which have been placed behind it for purposes of illuminating the cyclorama. A special *ground row*, called a "cove," often is painted the same color as the cyclorama, thus hiding an otherwise definite line between its base and the studio floor.

halo effect—A bright flare or bloom generally located around the perimeter of a highly reflective subject or object, which is the result of over illumination.

image-orthicon (I-O)—A highly sensitive television pickup tube which has become the standard tube in black and white broadcast cameras. This tube was also used for the luminance circuit in the early color broadcast television cameras.

incandescent lamp—A lamp used extensively in early television lighting instruments which employs a glowing filament to produce a desired level of brightness. Such lamps are characterized by a decrease in light output, and a change in color temperature with an increase in age.

key light—The principal source of light, generally a Fresnel spot, used to illuminate a subject. When properly placed, the *key* light illuminates approximately three-fourths of a subject's face, leaving the remaining one-fourth in dark shadow.

keystone effect—Distortion caused by a camera lens which has been placed off to one side, and at a height above or below that of an object being photographed. The end result is an object in which the perspective is distorted, or in the case of lettering, a tendency to run up or down hill to the left or right of the camera.

lag—A picture distortion characteristic of vidicon tubes where an object being photographed appears to smear or produce a following image as the camera is panned rapidly from one object or person to the next. Such lag can be reduced by increasing the intensity or light level of the acting area.

limbo—A special lighting technique characterized by a black background with a central middleground object or figure well illuminated in a full three-dimensional presentation.

matte print—A graphic, generally a photograph, which displays a dull surface finish thus causing little or no surface reflectance when illuminated.

modeling light—Light designed to bring out the three-dimensional qualities of a subject or object. Also, another name for the *key* light.

Plumbicon—The most common camera pickup tube used today in broadcast color cameras. The *Plumbicon* combines the characteristics of low lag with high sensitivity and is, therefore, utilized in both black and white and color broadcast cameras.

quartz-iodine lamp—A high intensity lamp generally used as standard equipment for today's television lighting instruments, so named because the filament is maintained in an iodine vapor atmosphere. Because the lamp does not change its color temperature with age, has a far greater illumination output than its incandescent counterpart, and is relatively small in size, it is ideally suited for color television.

rear projection screen—A transluscent plastic screen designed to facilitate the projection of 2 × 2 or 35mm slides it is placed behind. The slides are then televised from the front of the screen. The rear screen is often placed behind the subject, thus serving as a background device.

scoop—An oval television floodlamp made up of a light spreading parabolic reflector without a lens. Such an instrument projects a light, the edge of which is one-half the intensity of that found in the center of its pattern, thus providing an opportunity for overlapping lighting areas to create an even illumination of a cyclorama or other such flat surface.

scrim—A fine open weave fabric screen used in theatrical productions for the creation of visual illusions. Placement of light behind the scrim causes it to disappear, while a scene in the background remains in full view. Illumination of the scrim from the front causes it to appear, while the set located behind becomes invisible. Sometimes used in television for visual effects involving rolling the focus of a lens through a foreground *scrim* to a background scene.

silhouette—A special lighting technique characterized by a brightly illuminated background with a darkened foreground subject recognized only by its outline.

spill light—See ambient light.

subtractive color system—A system used to describe those colors possessed by such items as paint, dye, ink, or natural minerals, where the mixture of all colors results in the creation of a black pigment. Such a system is based upon the principle that each colored pigment absorbs those portions of the spectrum which it does not reflect.

telephoto lens—A television lens characterized by a comparatively shallow depth of field, a long focal length, and an ability to magnify objects located at great distances from the camera.

top light—A term applied to a *back* light which has been incorrectly positioned over the top of a subject's head at a steep 90° vertical angle. Such placement tends to decrease good modeling by throwing light on the top of a subject's head, often extending as far forward as the forehead and tip of the nose.

tungsten filament—The filament found in an incandescent lamp.

vidicon—A camera pickup tube used in both black and white and color television cameras possessing the quality of durability but lacking in the degree of sensitivity found in the I-O camera tube. The vidicon tube is used primarily in closed circuit television systems but was also employed extensively in the earliest broadcast color cameras in conjunction with the I-O tube.

Index